descant

Fifty Years

Betsy Colquitt

Louise Cowan

descant *Fifty Years*

※ THE LITERARY JOURNAL OF TCU

Edited by
Dave Kuhne,
Daniel E. Williams,
Charlotte Hogg, *and*
Charlotte Willis

TCU Press
Fort Worth

Copyright © 2008 TCU English Department

descant, fifty years : the literary journal of TCU / edited by Dave Kuhne ... [et al.].
    p. cm.
  ISBN 978-0-87565-348-8 (alk. paper)
  1. American literature–20th century. 2. American literature–21st century. 3. descant (Fort Worth, Tex.) I. Kuhne, Dave. II. descant (Fort Worth, Tex.)
  PS536.2F54 2008
  810.8'0054–dc22
                                2007038621

TCU Press
P.O. Box 298300
Fort Worth, TX 76129
817.257.7822

To order books: 800.826.8911

http://www.prs.tcu.edu/

Designed by Barbara Mathews Whitehead

Dedicated to

Betsy Colquitt

and

Louise Cowan

Contents

1 / *Introduction* by Dave Kuhne
5 / Betsy Colquitt—*descant: A Memoir*

PART 1: 1956-1969

11 / Bill Camfield—*Cricket From a Yellow Room*
14 / Betsy Colquitt—*Fish Caught*
15 / Albert Howard Carter and Ben Kimpel—*Translations from the "Triumphs" of Petrarch*
17 / Jim Corder—*The Man on the Square Meditates on the Urban Movement*
19 / Edsel Ford—*How I Live in a Drug Store*
21 / Charles Bukowski—*Many Ways*
22 / Anne Leaton—*The Sweet Waters of Asia*
23 / Daniel Garza—*Everybody Knows Tobie*
31 / William D. Barney—*The Killdeer Crying*
36 / Robert L. Flynn—*The Bad Time*
39 / Karl Shapiro—*What is Creative Writing? Or Playing Footsie with the Philistines*
59 / Robert Penn Warren—*Learning to Write*
70 / William A. Kittredge—*The Cove*
81 / Coleman Barks—*Yelling*
82 / J. M. Ferguson, Jr.—*Spending the Day*
96 / Denise Levertov—*Red Snow*
98 / Richard Snyder—*Sestina: Letters from a Girl in the Peace Corps*

PART 2: 1970-1989

103 / *Introduction* by Daniel E. Williams
105 / Colette Inez—*Remembered a Mustang She Rode to the South*
106 / Greg Kuzma—*The Porcupines*
107 / David Madden—*A Human Interest Death*
119 / Doris Betts—*Peripheral Vision*
120 / Walter McDonald—*Cam Rahn Bay Hospital Surgical Ward*
122 / David Bottoms—*The Door*
124 / Kelly Cherry—*Ashes to Syllables*
126 / Paul Ruffin—*Female Cousins at Thanksgiving*
128 / Annette Sanford—*Nobody Listens When I Talk*
132 / Pattiann Rogers—*How You Came*
133 / Joyce Carol Oates—*Poetics 105*
144 / D. C. Berry—*The Garbage Man*
146 / Lee Abbott—*Identify These Parts of the Body*
148 / Jerry Bradley—*Arrest*
149 / Tony Clark—*Minor Accident Near the Check-out Stand*
150 / Carol Coffee Reposa—*Hill Country Rest Home*
152 / Taylor Graham—*Bottles*
153 / Larry D. Thomas—*Herefords in Winter*

PART 3: 1990-2005

157 / *Introduction* by Charlotte Hogg
159 / Ulf Kirchdorfer—*Fish*
160 / Robert Wexelblatt—*We Lead Three Lives*
162 / Robert Coles—*In Sweden*
163 / Robert Parham—*Hurricane*
164 / Jill Patterson—*Any Minute*
173 / Clyde Edgerton—*Out of Rosehaven*
177 / R. S. Gwynn—*The Porch Swing*
178 / Andrew Hudgins—*Flamingos Have Arrived in Ashtabula*
180 / William Harrison—*Dove Season*
189 / John Byron Yarbrough—*Boiled White*
190 / Charles Harper Webb—*I Named My Cat "Keats"*
192 / Bruce Machart—*Where You Begin*
200 / Dana Roeser—*Land of the Lotus Eaters: Sea Island, Georgia*
202 / Ronald E. Moore—*The Real Funeral*
203 / Chris Ellery—*Bimaristan Arghun*
205 / Bonnie Hunter—*In a Cabin on the Cossatot River*
206 / Catherine McCraw—*Instead of a Wedding Dress*

207 / *Contributors*
213 / *Acknowledgments*

Introduction

In the early 1950s, TCU English professor Louise Cowan and her husband, Don Cowan, a physics professor who later became president of the University of Dallas, held meetings in their home with a group of creative writing students. In these meetings, the professors and students would discuss and analyze each other's creative endeavors. Louise Cowan had recently earned her Ph.D. at Vanderbilt and had published her dissertation on the Fugitives—the informal Vanderbilt literary society that had produced a journal by that name. The Fugitives included writers such as Allen Tate, John Crowe Ransom, and Robert Penn Warren; they became known as the "New Critics." The Cowans, along with Betsy Colquitt (whom they had known at Vanderbilt), Marjorie Dunlavy (future TCU English professor Marjorie Lewis), and other students in Cowan's creative writing class decided to launch a literary journal named *descant*. They chose the title of the journal from a line in a Yeats poem, "Speech After Long Silence." TCU English professor Mary Fisher enlisted her husband, business executive Beeman Fisher, to obtain funding for the early issues of the journal, and *descant* was born. As Colquitt notes in her memoir about *descant*, the journal benefited from the advice offered by the Cowans and the support and encouragement of TCU faculty such as Mabel Major, Lorraine Sherley, and Paul Dinkins. The TCU "critical discussion group" in those early days of *descant* included several authors who would go on to have impressive careers: Bill Camfield, the pioneering writer of children's television; Jim Corder, the TCU English professor who helped shape the emerging field of modern rhetoric and composition studies; and William D. Barney, who became Poet Laureate of Texas and whose poem, "The Killdeer Crying," won the Robert Frost Award.

The Cowans soon moved to Dallas to work at the newly founded University of Dallas, and the TCU English department appointed Betsy Colquitt to edit the journal. A glance at the table of contents of

descant

this anthology demonstrates that Betsy Colquitt, editor of *descant* until her retirement in 1996, had an uncanny eye for recognizing promising authors. As the journal grew and began to attract submissions from across Texas, Colquitt published early works by writers who would eventually establish national and international reputations: Charles Bukowski, William Kittredge, Denise Levertov, David Bottoms, Coleman Barks, Robert Flynn, Walt McDonald, Clyde Edgerton, and Joyce Carol Oates, among others.

During its first half century of publication, *descant* has shifted its focus and format several times. In its early decades, *descant* was not only a journal of poetry and short fiction but also a journal of the humanities, publishing translations of the classics, literary criticism, and creative nonfiction. Colquitt and her colleague at TCU, Mabel Major, who together organized the English department's annual creative writing celebration, often invited the keynote speakers of the weeklong celebration to publish their presentations in *descant.* Among these speakers were Karl Shapiro, who contributed an essay to *descant* in 1964, and Robert Penn Warren, who contributed to *descant* in 1965. More than forty years after their original appearances in the journal, the Shapiro and Penn essays remain important and insightful in terms of their discussion of writing and the place of arts in American culture. The tradition of inviting the keynote speakers of the annual creative writing celebration to submit to the journal was revived when William Harrison visited campus and contributed his outstanding story, "Dove Season," to *descant 2001*. And in recent years, the journal has begun publishing interviews with authors, such as Michael Mewshaw and Paul Ruffin, who have visited TCU.

Over the decades, the journal has moved from publishing three issues a year, to publishing two issues a year, to eventually, in 2000, becoming an annual publication. In the 1970s, the journal ceased publishing literary criticism and translations, and, in 1978, began offering an award for short fiction. The Frank O'Connor Award is a $500 prize given to the best short story published in an issue of *descant*. Colquitt was instrumental in bringing this award, endowed by a donor who wished to remain anonymous, to the journal when

Introduction

Quartet, which was edited by Richard Hauer Costa, ceased publication. In the 1990s, the journal began offering the Betsy Colquitt Award, another $500 prize, for the best poem in an issue. In 2003, Baskerville Publishers of Fort Worth initiated the $250 Baskerville Publishers Award, for an outstanding poem in an issue, and in 2005, an anonymous donor founded the $250 Gary Wilson Award, bringing the total awards to $1,500 per year. The Wilson award, for an outstanding story in an issue, is given in memory of Gary Wilson, a brilliant and talented translator and fiction writer in the MFA program at the University of Arkansas in the late 1970s. Wilson died of cancer shortly before completing his degree. The award series, which requires no entry or reading fee, is one reason why *descant* continues to receive thousands of submissions each year. When *descant* reaches the age of one hundred in 2055, I am confident that many of the winners of these awards, like many of the authors Betsy Colquitt published in the early decades of the journal's history, will have become recognized voices in American letters.

—Dave Kuhne

Betsy Colquitt

descant: A Memoir
—from *descant 2000*

Listed on the inside front cover of *descant*, *The Texas Christian University Literary Journal,* Fall 1956, Volume One, Number One, are the names of the forty-six donors who contributed the money needed to publish *descant*. Among the donors are most of the English faculty, several TCU trustees, former and current TCU students, and others, usually from Fort Worth, with an interest in literature and little magazines. Though I don't remember how much time this fundraising required, for many years, donors and fundraising were essential to *descant's* existence. So too were subscribers, who paid $1.50 for the three-issue volumes. When the journal became a quarterly in 1964, a subscription cost $2.00. Such charges seem improbably low today, but publication and postage costs were much smaller then.

Like most first issues of little magazines, the initial issue of *descant* includes an editorial. Placed on page one, the editorial outlines the journal's purpose and its origin. The editorial is predictably lofty about *descant's* aims and optimistic about their achievement. Defining a literary journal as "a medium of presentation and comment" concerned with "the state of letters," the editorial asserts that such a journal can "approach that concern with a conscious integrity denied the more popular media" and thus can "advance the state of letters" by publishing writings that are "orthodox or experimental, primitive or polished, spontaneous or deliberate." By doing so, *descant* can "hew out its character according to the convictions and abilities of its editors."

Titled "By Way of Introduction," the editorial also notes that all writings in the issue are from members of a "critical discussion group" at TCU that, since 1953, had read and critiqued stories and poems by group members. This close interaction between editors and writers is expected "to continue" even though "future contributors will not be limited to this group." The editorial concludes, "Because it is a college journal, it has upon it the stamp of thought, for we who have committed ourselves to a belief in man's intelligence believe that only after much thought, much talk, and much silence can we '*descant* upon the supreme theme of art and song.'"

All staff members who worked the first issue were TCU undergraduates and graduate students who had participated in the discussion group. Since TCU required faculty advisers for all student publications, Mabel Major and Louise Cowan, both prominent members of the English faculty, agreed to accept this responsibility.

Professor Major, a member of the TCU faculty from 1919 to 1963 when she retired, taught Shakespeare and other Renaissance courses as well as courses in Southwestern Literature. Louise Cowan and her husband, Don Cowan, joined the TCU faculty in 1953, she in English and he in physics.

The Cowans, whom I met when I was a TCU junior, and I became friends. They influenced me greatly as they have hundreds of others over the years, and I remain most grateful to them and also to two of my TCU English teachers, Lorraine Sherley and Paul Dinkins. The four of them became my mentors. Encouraged by them to think of college teaching as a possible career in spring 1947 as I was finishing my BA at TCU, I applied to graduate programs. Paul strongly recommended Vanderbilt, where he earned his doctorate, and his reference letter for me accounts for my receiving a scholarship. The Cowans also applied to Vanderbilt. Though my stay in Nashville was limited to the 1947–48 academic year when I earned an MA, the Cowans spent several years in Nashville, and both completed doctorates there. Louise was encouraged by her Vanderbilt professors to choose as her dissertation project an examination of the Fugitive poets, a group of students, faculty, and townspeople who created a literary society that began during the last years of World War I and continued until about 1925. Individually and collectively, the Fugitives were among the earliest contributors to the literary movement usually called "The Southern Renaissance."

Though this long digression about the Cowans may seem unconnected to *descant*'s beginnings, it isn't. The Fugitives became the model for the "critical discussion group" the Cowans founded at TCU in 1953, and from her dissertation, which is one of the earliest scholarly studies of the Fugitive writers and which LSU published in 1959, Louise Cowan knew the benefits that the Fugitive writers gained from group meetings and discussion. Like the TCU group, the Fugitives included students, faculty, and a few townspeople who wrote or had an interest in writing. Like the TCU discussion group, the Vanderbilt group also published a literary magazine, *The Fugitive*. Like *descant*, *The Fugitive* was supported by donations, usually from Nashville townspeople, and by subscriptions. Vanderbilt never funded the journal, which published eighteen issues over the course of its life of three years: 1922 through 1925. TCU has been more generous with *descant*, which since 1965 has had some university funding. The magazine also benefits from a couple of endowments given to TCU with the requirement that their earnings be assigned to the magazine.

In 1959, the Cowans accepted faculty appointments at the University of Dallas, and the TCU discussion group that the Cowans and a few others helped to create and maintain had dispersed as student groups necessarily do. Meanwhile, an increase in submissions to *descant* meant that the interaction between writers and editors that the first issue set as a goal became more and more elusive. Increasingly, *descant* published more manuscripts from writers with no immediate connection to TCU or to this area, and the submissions often came from writers who had numerous publications.

Though my connection to the original student group and to the beginning of *descant* obviously came from my friendship with the Cowans, it also came from my interest in poetry and fiction and in little magazines (where I sometimes published). When I became a member of the TCU English Department in 1954, I was assigned the job of editing *descant*. As time passed, *descant* became better known, grew in reputation, and gained some financial stability. Though printing and mailing costs greatly increased over the years, the magazine was always solvent, and that it's alive and well after four decades amazes and pleases me.

I think too that though *descant* wasn't, and isn't now, a deliberately regional journal, it has helped bring attention to writers in Texas and the Southwest. Contributions by Walter McDonald, Dave Hickey, William Barney, Carolyn Osborn, Tony Clark, and many others belong in this category. At times, the magazine was lucky in accepting works from writers who later gained national reputations. Among these are Anne Tyler and Clyde Edgerton, both of whom published early stories in *descant*.

Being associated with the magazine from its beginning until 1996 when I retired makes me feel an almost maternal pride in the publication, which has also been fortunate in the many others who've worked on the journal. The English department was generous in assigning student assistants to help with the journal. Moreover, department secretaries such as Phyllis Drake, and more recently, Claudia Knott, willingly helped with the many details publication involves. Colleagues too were generous in taking on editorial tasks. Among the most important were Harry Opperman, David Vanderwerken, Stanley Trachtenberg, and Steve Sherwood who served as fiction editors. I'm also grateful to Neil Easterbrook, who, with a cadre of students, edited the journal just after I retired. That this editorial process replicated the journal's beginnings is also fitting. Now, and, I hope, for many years to come, *descant*'s editor is Dave Kuhne, and with the assistance of his poetry editor, Lynn Risser, I'm certain the journal will continue to thrive.

Though *descant*'s forty-four years of publication doesn't rival the longevity of little magazines like *Poetry: A Magazine of Verse*, which began in 1915, forty-four years isn't bad for a little magazine that began with great hopes and ambitions. In those years, some hopes and ambitions were realized, and the journal has had a modest success or two along the way. *descant 2000*, a special issue devoted to outstanding Texas writing, is yet another of those successes.

descant

THE TEXAS CHRISTIAN UNIVERSITY LITERARY JOURNAL
VOLUME ONE, NUMBER ONE FALL, 1956

1956–1969

Bill Camfield

Cricket From a Yellow Room
—from *descant* 1.1 (Fall 1956)

It is very early, and several crickets and I are up. They are not, insofar as I know, contemplating time and place. They are chirping, a particular aptitude of their species. I am contemplating, an aptitude of mine. They shall soon go back to sleep, and I cannot. They have a decided advantage.

What place is this? Which place? I am in a chair, which is in a room of a house, located on a street in a neighborhood of a city in the northern portion of a state of one of the largest nations of the earth, which is a planet. This planet, I am told, is located in a solar system of a galaxy, which is a subdivision of a Universe. Supposedly there is just one of these. I cannot disprove that, at least from this chair. The crickets do not seem disposed to discuss the problem.

Am I to say, then, that I am in several places? Why not? It gives me unique advantage insofar as the crickets are concerned. As a member of the homo-sapiens fraternity, I am able to consider, in ever widening spirals of imagination, all the places occupied by my chair. I can think of the hardness of the chair itself, the yellowness of the room, the smallness of the house, the desirability of the neighborhood, the smell of the city, the politics of the state, the wealth of the nation, the diversity of the Earth. From this chair, I can even see much of the Universe, and indulge in interplanetary worry. Crickets, they say, cannot think or worry. Pitiful, lowly beings!

There is much I can do about this place, or at least some of these places. At this time, in this place, I have what is called power. The chair is mine, and I can use it, destroy it, or dispose of it for profit. As the circle widens, however, my influence regresses. In this room, at this moment, I can do pretty much as I please. In this house, my sovereignty is halved. In the city, the nation, the Earth, I would begin to use ever-remote decimals to estimate my power, or my influence, or

descant

my importance. I suppose, then, that what Is Sovereign is relative to the place we think of being in. Like the aperture of a lens, we can widen or reduce the angle of our imagination, think of the place we occupy and make ourselves supreme or minute, vain or humble. We are in many places at once, and we can contemplate one of them or all of them and be right.

I wonder about the cricket? If he thinks of his place, does he consider the blade of grass next to him and feel that he is the supreme creature of the Universe? Or, does he look up at the heavens and feel his finitude? Is his aperture fixed, so that he knows what he really is? Or, is it adjustable, like ours, so that he questions his real importance? Does he have knowledge? Or does he have speculations? Is he an idealist? Or is he a realist?

Since I am a human being, and to a certain degree obligated to consider all other creatures (non-angelic) as inferior, I shall accept the findings of the research psychologists (also human beings in the majority) and classify the cricket as a lower biological form who happens to have the privilege to return to bed. I am sure he won't mind.

An arbitrary decision such as this is necessary, I suppose, to maintain sanity. This is another unique problem of our species. Our room can be a prison or a haven. It can be both at the same time.

The cricket has stopped chirping and turned in, and I hear the man next door stumble into his kitchen and break a glass. Is it possible that the crickets have turned over the controls to men again? We are now ready to stretch and shave and go about the business of running the Creation. When the dawn comes, things seem suddenly to snap back into a heartening focus, and this time and this place suddenly fill with the problems of living. Philosophy yields to the tedious task of working our way through another day. Crickets and their problems dissolve with the dawn, and men can begin to putter.

This room is now a familiar fixture in a routine existence. It is a place where I keep a typewriter and some books, a chair and a few pictures. It has a view of my backyard which I must mow, and is a place where I keep some bills, which I must pay. It is not only my room, it is our room.

There are a steam iron and a sewing cabinet and a few strap pins on the floor. My wife sews here. It is in this room that she makes pleasant frocks and knits bright mittens. It is in this room that I make little stories and commune with crickets at inhuman hours. This is our warm, yellow room with the gray ceiling and the outcast green chair. This is the room where I am comfortable and safe and sovereign.

Excuse me, if I sounded lyric about the hour. The early morning is the prime of day. It is intoxicating to watch a dawn from a familiar room. It is a daily adventure to sit in the quiet, smoking and stirring coffee and watching for the world to be born outside the window. The birth is sudden, and you must watch for that precise instant when it is tomorrow. If you doze, you will miss it.

Time is awesome before dawn. It seems endless and infinite and animate. A watch or a clock seems to have no relation to it. But, when it is light, the world can run in mathematical precision, meshing hours and minutes and arranging them orderly into days.

It is a pleasant luxury to sit in my room before dawn and think of time and place in wide circles. It is a joy, I am sure, for the cricket to sit outside my window, diligently employed at his chirping. His skill is admirable and his patience and persistence is to be commended.

But now that he has finished, and it is day, time becomes the master of me. Time can no longer be contemplated but must be obeyed. The soft hush of pre-dawn becomes the electric pause before the dash for dusk. My room becomes suddenly the place where I must dress and tie my shoes and swallow the coffee that's too hot to drink. My room will wait until the evening in silent fidelity. I will leave it in a moment and it will be just a room in a house in a neighborhood in a fair-sized Universe. Goodbye, yellow room. Sleep well, fortunate cricket, may I borrow your Universe today?

descant

Betsy Colquitt

Fish Caught
—from *descant* 2.1 (Fall 1957)

They say the fish mouth-caught can feel no pain
from hook embedded in cold flesh and blood,
but learns caughtness as gills gall in water
crossed too fast. And we in opaque elements
learn not see the lash, chain, thread
of fisher whose catch leaves most freedom
till firmly fixed, we are line pulled,
bled, and bound from our dense substances;

pulled by cutting, galling, scraping to bright pier,
taken like fish from our habitat though
not to be parched or drowned with air;
rather are blinded with dazzling so to see,
smothered by love to make breath, devoured
body and blood to feast spirit; in violent sacrament,
dyed by stains indelible to birth our element
outlasting our elements, caught and galled
by fisher wise.

Albert Howard Carter
and Ben Kimpel

Translations from the "Triumphs" of Petrach
—from *descant* 3.2 (Winter 1959)

I. That time my sighs became renewed
Through the sweet memory of that day
That bore such lengthy martyrdom
The sun between the horns of Taurus
Had grown in warmth and the Titan's daughter
Had scattered frost from his customed haunts,
Love, scorns, plaints, and the seasons
Had led me back to the covert place
Where tired hearts lay down their burdens.
Here on the grass, worn with weeping,
Conquered by sleep, I saw a brightness
And within great sorrow but brief joy.
I saw a victorious and potent leader
Like one of those, who on the course,
Drives his triumphant chariot to glory.

II. (And the shade of Laura said to me:)
'Your joy has blinded you to the flight of time;
I see Aurora from her golden bed
Lead back the day to mortals, and the Sun,
Risen breast-high in the ocean,
Comes to part us, whence my sorrow;
If you've more to say, speak briefly,
Measuring your words against the time.'
'Whatever I've suffered has made for me,'
I said, 'this sweet hour the sweeter,
But living without you, will be the bitterer.
And so, madonna, tell me whether

descant

I'm to follow you soon or late.'
She, going, answered, 'You will stay
Without me many years on earth.'
When Death had triumphed over her,
Who'd always triumphed over me,
Whose sun he'd stolen from our world,
He left, pitiless in his guilt,
Pale to sight, horrid, and proud,
He, who'd spent the light of her beauty.
    Looking then across the grass I saw
Coming from the other side, the spirit
Who keeps men from the tomb, alive, that is.
As the star of love at the break of day
Comes from the East before the Sun
Who loves to have her for companion,
Thus she came. And oh, where's to be found
A master who could wholly describe
What I would say in simple words?

III. These triumphs, the five, we see on earth,
And in the end, if God so wills,
The sixth we are to see above.
When Time who readily undoes us all
And Death will both be dead together
And those who merit Fame, which Time
Has spent and lucid faces which Death
Has paled, will flower and grow again
In deathless beauty and eternal fame.
And she for whom the world weeps
Through my tongue, my tired pen—
If sight of her on earth made us happy
What can it be to see her again in heaven?

Jim Corder

The Man on the Square Meditates on the Urban Movement
—from *descant* 4.1 (Fall 1959)

I do not know the land I long for,
Neither bird nor bush, rock, tree, nor vine.
Like the asthmatic boy, strong for
A season (the judgment of his time and mine),
I stifle in the dust of weeds and time.

Plow time and pick time he grows pale.
As the wind comes up from the north and west,
Driving over alien earth, it cannot fail
To reach him; even at our sanitary best
Plow time and pick time he cannot rest.

(Would Wordsworth, I wonder, preface while wheezing,
Or how could Shelley be blithe while sneezing?)

The lore and the land are gone. We made a trap
In time that catches us away from earth
(Though I sometimes threaten a summer camping trip).
A crop grows about the house of my birth,
But I don't know its name and can't judge its worth.

Yet I prize it all, and the arrowhead on my desk,
The bolt of an old gun on the floor.
My father and his father once knew the risk
Of rain. They hurried the land with poor
Crops, moved to town, got credit at the store,

descant

And now I do not know the land,
Though I remember stories that my father told—
How a bridge was built, how a certain horse ran,
How he caught a snake when he wasn't very old,
How he built a fire when the morning was cold.

But where is the story that I will tell?
When the wind comes up from across the plains
Whipping the sand along, it takes its toll
Of me as well. I do not know the feel of grain,
And I have never ached with that worry of rain.

Only with slow steps I take my way
To the quiet square and whittle the day.

Edsel Ford

How I Live in a Drug Store
—from *descant* 5.3 (Spring 1961)

I live in a drug store.
They let me live here, though I do not pay rent.
I have my visions and I write my poems here.
People come in and look curiously and spend their money,
though I do not get any of it.
They ask in awed whispers is he queer or what?
and they say he is what, but what they don't say.
The spiders have spun me a beard because
I have lived here so long
between the Gillette Blue Blades and the Lectric Shave;
the spiders have gullivered me into the back booth
where I stare at teething rings and the feet of people
limping toward the pharmacy.

Once I was all high-pitched boy and I drank Dr Pepper
in this booth at the noon-hour, kneeing a girl
who wore red bloomers and got away with it,
a girl who kneed me back and made my face turn red;
once I sat here and read the nickel comic books.
But there are no nickel comics any more,
and the girl in the red bloomers writes me once a year
from New York City where her father is glad to keep her,
though I would guess from the talk I hear
that others keep her, too.

descant

Once I was pregnant with the need to stare,
to hear, to know, to write about it all.
Now you must look again to tell that I am breathing,
for the spiders have webbed my eyes that the moths
do not flicker round them as they did,
and the ugly rumors of the times have sealed
my inner ear.

I live in a drug store.
People slurp sodas here, and they buy poison;
and one little boy stole a nickel tablet once:
that was the time I stirred. I saw the moths
wheeling about his tow head like a halo.
I told the manager, who sent the boy
bawling on his way. And when they set
a cup of coffee before me, waving away my nickel,
I drank it down as fast as I could
like hemlock.

Charles Bukowski

Many Ways
–from *descant* 6.1 (Fall 1961)

if you have read your Hemingway
or even if you haven't read your Hemingway,
and it's best to get it straight in your own way:
there are many ways to die.
the Mexican way to die is best with bulls and sunlight,
or as Lorca, the Spanish way, one lone man in the way
of dark horses; or the American way:
walking up hills behind the man in front;
or is it   our way   dying ahead of time
dying again and again so that when they
shut the door   no shadow   no sound
and the hedges and the thorns of the town
will cry only.

descant

Anne Leaton

The Sweet Waters of Asia
—from *descant* 6.3 (Spring 1962)

In Mahmet the Turk they are subterranean
and accompany his bones to pray
that the Bosphorus may remain as blue
as the limpid eyes of fish
or the heavens over Üsküdar;
Accompany his flesh its way
to rhetoric within the bowels
of Empire ladies;
Wash the roots of his eyes.

When the wind is out of the north's bitter throat
anchors fall heavily through ice
and crisply in the dark
birds cry.

The current moves
and in the columns of Mahmet the waters rise
until white birds traverse his eyes
and in their movement
shape the motions of his brain.

Daniel Garza

Everybody Knows Tobie
—from *descant* 7.3 (Spring 1963)

When I was thirteen years old my older brother, Tobie, had the town newspaper route. Everyone in the town knew him well because he had been delivering their papers for a year and a half. Tobie used to tell me that he had the best route of all because his customers would pay promptly each month, and sometimes, he used to brag that the nice people of the town would tip him a quarter or maybe fifty cents at the end of the month because he would trudge up many stairs to deliver the paper personally.

The other newspaper boys were not as lucky as Tobie because sometimes their customers would not be at home when they went by to collect payment for that month's newspaper, or maybe at the end of the month the customers would just try to avoid the paper boys to keep from paying.

Yes, Tobie had it good. The biggest advantage, I thought, that Tobie had over all the newspaper boys was that he knew the gringos of the town so well that he could go into a gringo barber shop and get a haircut without having the barber tell him to go to the Mexican barber in our town or maybe just embarrassing him in front of all the gringo customers in the shop as they often did when chicano cotton pickers came into their places during the fall months.

The gringo barbers of my town were careful whom they allowed in their shops during the cotton harvest season in the fall. September and October and cotton brought chicanos from the south to the north of Texas where I lived, and where the cotton was sometimes plentiful and sometimes scarce. Chicanos is what we say in our language, and it is slang among our people. It means the Mexicans of Texas. These chicano cotton pickers came from the Rio Grande Valley in South Texas, and sometimes, even people from Mexico made the

descant

trip to the north of Texas. All these chicanos came to my little town in which many gringos lived, and a few of us spoke both English and Spanish.

When the chicanos came to my town on Saturdays after working frightfully in the cotton fields all week, they would go to the town market for food, and the fathers would buy candy and ice cream for their flocks of little black-headed ones. The younger ones, the *jovenes*, would go to the local movie house. And then maybe those who had never been to the north of Texas before would go to the gringos' barbershops for haircuts not knowing that they would be refused. The gringo barbers would be very careful not to let them come too close to their shops because the regular gringo customers would get mad, and sometimes they would curse the chicanos.

"Hell, it's them damn pepper bellies again. Can't seem to get rid of 'em in the fall," the prejudiced gringos of my town would say. Some of the nicer people would only become uneasy at seeing so many chicanos with long, black, greasy hair wanting haircuts.

The barbers of the town liked Tobie, and they invited him to their shops for haircuts. Tobie said that the barbers told him that they would cut his hair because he did not belong to that group of people who came from the south of Texas. Tobie understood. And he did not argue with the barbers because he knew how chicanos from South Texas were, and how maybe gringo scissors would get all greasy from cutting their hair.

During that fall Tobie encouraged me to go to the gringos' place for a haircut. "Joey, when are you going to get rid of that mop of hair?" he asked.

"I guess I'll get rid of it when Mr. Lopez learns how to cut flat-tops."

"Golly, Joey, Mr. Lopez is a good ole guy and all that, but if he doesn't know how to give flat-tops then you should go to some other barber for flat-tops. Really, Kid-brother, that hair looks awful."

"Yeah, but I'm afraid."

"Afraid of what?" Tobie asked.

"I'm afraid the barber will mistake me for one of those guys from South Texas and run me out of his shop."

"Oh, piddle," Tobie said. "Mr. Brewer . . . you know, the barber who cuts my hair . . . is a nice man, and he'll cut your hair. Just tell him you're my kid-brother."

I thought about this new adventure for several days, and then on a Saturday, when there was no school, I decided on the haircut at Mr. Brewer's. I hurriedly rode my bike to town and parked it in the alley close to the barbershop. As I walked into the shop, I noticed that all of a sudden the gringos inside stopped their conversation and looked at me. The shop was silent for a moment. I thought then that maybe this was not too good and that I should leave. I remembered what Tobie had told me about being his brother, and about Mr. Brewer being a nice man. I was convinced that I belonged in the gringo barbershop.

I found an empty chair and sat down to wait my turn for a haircut. One gringo customer sitting next to me rose and explained to the barber that he had to go to the courthouse for something. Another customer left without saying anything. And then one, who was dressed in dirty coveralls and a faded khaki shirt, got up from Mr. Brewer's chair and said to him, "Say, Tom, looks like you got yourself a little tamale to clip."

Mr. Brewer smiled only.

My turn was next, and I was afraid. But I remembered again that this was all right because I was Tobie's brother, and everybody liked Tobie. I went to Mr. Brewer's chair. As I started to sit down, he looked at me and smiled a nice smile.

He said, "I'm sorry, Sonny, but I can't cut your hair. You go to Mr. Lopez's. He'll cut your hair."

Mr. Brewer took me to the door and pointed the way to Lopez's barbershop. He pointed with his finger and said, "See, over there behind that service station. That's his place. You go there. He'll clip your hair."

Tears were welling in my eyes. I felt a lump in my throat. I was too choked up to tell him I was Tobie's brother, and that it was all right to cut my hair. I only looked at him as he finished giving directions. He smiled again and patted me on the back. As I left, Mr. Brewer said, "Say hello to Mr. Lopez for me, will you, Sonny?"

descant

I did not turn back to look at Mr. Brewer. I kept my head bowed as I walked to Mr. Lopez's because tears filled my eyes, and these tears were tears of hurt to the pride and confidence which I had slowly gained in my gringo town.

I thought of many things as I walked slowly. Maybe this was a foolish thing which I had done. There were too many gringos in the town, and too few of us who lived there all the year long. This was a bad thing because the gringos had the right to say yes or no, and we could only follow what they said. It was useless to go against them. It was foolish. But I was different from the chicanos who came from the south, not much different. I did live in the town the ten months of the year when the other chicanos were in the South or in Mexico. Then I remembered what the barber had told my brother about the South Texas people, and why the gringo customers had left while I was in Mr. Brewer's shop. I began to understand. But it was very hard for me to realize that even though I had lived among gringos all of my life that I still had to go to my own people for such things as haircuts. Why wouldn't gringos cut my hair? I was clean. My hair was not long and greasy.

I walked into Mr. Lopez's shop. There were many chicanos sitting in the chairs and even on the floor waiting their turn for a haircut. Mr. Lopez paused from his work as he saw me enter and said, "Sorry, Joey, full up. Come back in a couple of hours."

I shrugged my shoulders and said O.K. As I started to leave I remembered what Mr. Brewer had told me to say to Mr. Lopez. "Mr. Lopez," I said, and all the chicanos, the ones who were waiting, turned and looked at me with curious eyes. "Mr. Brewer told me to tell you hello."

Mr. Lopez shook his head approvingly, not digesting the content of my statement. The chicanos looked at me again and began to whisper among themselves. I did not hear, but I understood.

I told Mr. Lopez that I would return later in the day, but I did not because there would be other chicanos wanting haircuts on Saturday. I could come during the week when he had more time, and when all the chicanos would be in the fields working.

I went away feeling rejected both by the gringos and even my people, the entire world I knew.

Back in the alley where my bike was parked I sat on the curb for a long while thinking how maybe I did not fit into this town. Maybe my place was in the south of Texas where there were many of my kind of people, and where there were more chicano barbershops and less gringo barbers. Yes, I thought, I needed a land where I could belong to one race. I was so concerned with myself that I did not notice a chicano, a middle-aged man dressed in a new chambray shirt and faded denim pants, studying me.

He asked, *"Que paso, Chamaco?"*

"Nada," I answered.

"Maybe the cotton has not been good for you this year."

"No, Señor. I live here in the town."

And then the chicano said, "Chico, I mistook you for one of us."

Suddenly the chicano became less interested in me and walked away unconcerned.

I could not have told him that I had tried for a haircut at the gringo's because he would have laughed at me, and called me a *pocho*, a chicano who prefers gringo ways. These experienced chicanos knew the ways of the gringos in the north of Texas.

After the chicano had left me, I thought that maybe these things which were happening to me in the town would all pass in a short time. The entire cotton crop would soon be harvested, and the farmers around my town would have it baled and sold. Then the chicanos would leave the north of Texas and journey back to their homes in the Valley in the south and to Mexico.

My town would be left alone for ten more months of the year, and in this time everything and everybody would be all right again. The gringo barbers would maybe think twice before sending me to Mr. Lopez's.

Early in November the last of the cotton around my town had been harvested. The people of South Texas climbed aboard their big trucks with tall sideboards and canvas on the top to shield the sun, and they began their long journey to their homes in the border country.

descant

The streets of the little town were now empty on Saturday.

A few farmers came to town on Saturday and brought their families to do their shopping, still the streets were quiet and empty.

In my home there was new excitement for me. Tobie considered leaving his newspaper route for another job, one that would pay more money. And I thought that maybe he would let me take over his route. This was something very good. By taking his route I would know all the gringos of the town, and maybe . . . maybe then the barbers would invite me to their shops as they had invited Tobie.

At supper that night I asked Tobie if he would take me on his delivery for a few days, and then let me deliver the newspaper on my own.

Tobie said, "No, Joey. You're too young to handle money. Besides, the newspaper bag would be too heavy for you to carry on your shoulder all over town. No, I think I'll turn the route over to Red."

My father was quiet during this time, but soon he spoke, "Tobie, you give the route to Joey. He knows about money. And he needs to put a little muscle on his shoulders."

The issue was settled.

The next day Tobie took me to the newspaper office. Tobie's boss, a nice elderly man wearing glasses, studied me carefully, scratched his white head, and then asked Tobie, "Well, what do you think?"

"Oh," Tobie said, "I told him he was too young to handle this job, but he says he can do it."

"Yes, sir," I butted in enthusiastically.

Tobie's boss looked at me and chuckled, "Well, he's got enough spunk."

He thought some more.

Tobie spoke, "I think he'll make you a good delivery boy, sir."

A short silence followed while Tobie's boss put his thoughts down on a scratch pad on his desk.

Finally, the boss said, "We'll give him a try, Tobie." He looked at me. "But, Young 'un, you'd better be careful with that money. It's your responsibility."

"Yes, sir," I gulped.

"O.K., that's settled," the boss said.

Tobie smiled and said, "Sir, I'm taking him on my delivery for a few days so he can get the hang of it, and then I'll let him take it over."

The boss agreed. I took his hand and shook it and promised him that I would do my extra best. Then Tobie left, and I followed behind.

In a few days I was delivering the *Daily News* to all the gringos of the town, and also, to Mr. Brewer.

Each afternoon, during my delivery, I was careful not to go into Mr. Brewer's with the newspaper. I would carefully open the door and drop the paper in. I did this because I thought that maybe Mr. Brewer would remember me, and this might cause an embarrassing incident. But I did this a very few times because one afternoon Mr. Brewer was standing at the door. He saw me. I opened the door and quickly handed him the newspaper, but before I could shut the door he said, "Say, Sonny, aren't you the one I sent to Mr. Lopez's a while back?"

"Yes, sir," I said.

"Why'd you stay around here? Didn't your people go back home last week? You do belong to 'em, don't you?"

"No, sir." I said. "I live here in the town."

"You mean to say you're not one of those . . . ?"

"No, sir."

"Well, I'll be durned." He paused and thought. "You know, Sonny, I have a young Meskin boy who lives here in town come to this here shop for haircuts every other Saturday. His name is . . . durn, can't think of his name to save my soul . . ."

"Tobie?"

"Yeah, yeah, that's his name. Fine boy. You know him?"

"Yes, sir. He's my older brother."

Then Mr. Brewer's eyes got bigger in astonishment, "'Well, I'll be doubly durned." He paused and shook his head unbelievingly. "And I told you to go to Mr. Lopez's. Why didn't you speak up and tell me you was Tobie's brother? I would a put you in that there chair and clipped you a pretty head of hair."

"Oh, I guess I forgot to tell you," I said.

"Well, from now on, Sonny, you come to this here shop, and I'll cut your hair."

"But what about your customers? Won't they get mad?"

"Naw. I'll tell 'em you're Tobie's brother, and everything will be all right. Everybody in town knows Tobie, and everybody likes him."

Then a customer walked into the barbershop. He looked at Mr. Brewer, and then at me, and then at my newspaper bag. And then the gringo customer smiled a nice smile at me.

"Well, excuse me, Sonny, got a customer waitin'. Remember now, come Saturday, and I'll clip your hair."

"O.K., Mr. Brewer. Bye."

Mr. Brewer turned and said good-bye.

As I continued my delivery I began to chuckle small bits of contentment to myself because Mr. Brewer had invited me to his shop for haircuts, and because the gringo customer had smiled at me, and because now all the gringos of the town would know me and maybe accept me.

Those incidents which had happened to me during the cotton harvest in my town: Mr. Brewer sending me to Mr. Lopez's for the haircut, and the chicano cotton picker avoiding me after discovering that I was not one of his people, and the gringo customers leaving Mr. Brewer's barbershop because of me; all seemed so insignificant. And now I felt that delivering the *Daily News* to the businessmen had given me a place among them, and all because of the fact that everybody in my town knew Tobie.

William D. Barney

The Killdeer Crying
—from *descant* 7.3 (Spring 1963)

        He wasn't easy fooled. Not I was fooling
anybody, it was more deciphering. That was it:
he had me working shinnery and trash, going
toward bedrock and toward bottom. You know the way
a fox lays down a scent and then sits back
to see who follows.

                      White galls. The white galls
of limestone hills. In this calloused land
a spring of separate dickcissels.

                            He said
he liked living up there. First, he liked living,
but next he liked living up there in the cedar
and the mesquite. Where he could look out long,
far over the flats. No, not the looking down, it wasn't that.
It was the headlands—that's his word—the headlands
rising up from a barren floor.

                      He wasn't easy fooled.
I ventured out this notion of mine, just to see
what he'd respond. He was suspicious. First, why
did I come up there to nitpick him? An old law-hound
gets a look about him, so nobody takes him
for telling truth. He must have seen me squinting
hard at his view.

descant

      I say more probable the stuttering,
the subrosa rasping, the white-undersided remarking
of cottonwoods. Again they don't sound
like riffles, however they sound. Everyone knows
it takes but a tickle of wind and they tambourine.

Why say he fancied cedar? It's not worth
a shadow in the moon. It's of a color fit
for Hell, if anything'll grow there.

          He said he heard
it just the same. And he looked at me with his fogged-
over eye, stared into me, it was. I know what I hear,
he says. More than one man I've talked into lowering
his sights, and so I talked and so I talked, but never once
did he let down his eyes. They kept sweeping blue and cold
as if they'd turn to beacons.

        Not the sound
itself. But the irritant of them. Maybe it was
the dickcissels. One of them listens like another
over and over at intervals. A mind could grow
monotonous with them all about.

          So I said
wait, you can catch that smell coming off out there.
Even it smells like it. But he wasn't to be trapped
by anything so simple. He just looked pitying
and maybe a little angry. Like some dried lizard,
bony and gaunt and being strangled by the climate
and soon to be extinct.

William D. Barney

In the middles
of still nights I have come out here, middles with
the white moon lowered down like someone set to read
the print of earth with a single candle, I have come
out here on these limestone slabs, these galls, these slant
thick scabs that cap some hidden sore, I have come out
on nights of the moon, thinking to test my senses,
summer and winter, with leaves on the mesquite and none,
but it makes no difference, I hear that eternal sound,
that slow successive sound. And all around the great
bare capes you could put signals on.

                Cedar does things
to a person. A man oughn't live out alone in the cedars.
I say that.

     What about pathology? A clot caught on a master node?
some common physical reason? Simplification is a blessing
in this mangled world. I, I believe in botany
and very simple explanations for almost anything.
Oh, we don't know the explanations. I didn't say that.
All we know is, there must be explanations. But men
won't have it easy. They must have mystery, or they shrivel.

Times come to us all. Plowing I've had the feel
of being an ancient snail, scrawling along on the bottom
of a huge bowl, a tremendous basin. Not that I ever
heard anything. But you could get to where you heard.

This farmer, he heard a bell, it was a cowbell,
nobody else ever could hear. People kept wondering where
he got all that thin milk.

descant

                      Supposing he says he hears?
Who's to object? This is fearful free country, and free speech
includes the inner earful, don't it? Trouble with saying that
is I don't feel so much persuaded. Are they entitled
to the same protection as the rest of us? They need more.

The killdeer, then. The killdeer, crying in the uplands,
on the sandbars, in the stony fields. The killdeer crying
for all the world like sea-lost gulls.

                            I know what I hear.
The blunt hills beat like smitten tines. What I hear
is long before, an echo of a primitive strain.
But echo is too quick a meaning. This is force cast back
on us from olden time, a sound that struck the farthest star
and now returns to shudder us.

                      Nobody even mentioned guilt?
Deep sin has sharpened a many ear. I say a sight is wrong
when men look everywhere for explanation save
in the inside heart. I hold with the friends of Job.
Affliction is in the heart.

                      It's not my chosen profession. It's
counterwise to all my years, this way. The good Lord
mercifully matches me with the wicked. I've never stumbled
finding which way to catch them jumping. But the innocent
are too spry. What tricks will I use on the innocent?
The sound is dead as fossils in this stone,
I said. What is your play? What do you look to gain
making a show before men? What's it to gain, he said.

William D. Barney

                                             All
this talk while a man is sick, to death, to death,
dangerous death; and the sickness not so fearful
as the talk.

    I've come out here after ice-storms
with everything bowed down and caught in a silent claw,
the cedars even, nothing moving but a once-in-a-while
robin anxious for berries, Lord, you know how these hills
glaze over with a sheet of ice a quarter-inch thick
sometimes in February. Yes. I've come out then,
and if I stopped and held my peace a heartbeat I could hear it,
long and heavy and unhurried and just as sure as sunlight
it would go on like it always. Why should I say
less than a truth happens within me?

                             The killdeer
on the gravel bars remember.

                          The cedar thrives on this
gray rock, these hills, not cottonwood.

                             The headlands:
that was his own word.

                 I know what I hear.

                            He wasn't easy fooled
and it's not my chosen
            In botany I believe.
                                 The killdeer
crying, the killdeer crying like gulls.

Robert L. Flynn

The Bad Time
—from *descant* 8.1 (Fall 1963)

He sat on the edge of the bunk, his head down, his arms hanging loosely between his knees, shivering uncontrollably from time to time. He had been like this all night. He had not eaten yesterday and he felt weak and empty inside. He had tried to eat, but his throat would not accept the food. His head ached dully, and his mind turned slowly, distractedly, without focusing.

When he heard them coming down the corridor, their steps regular, yet casual, he could not believe it was time. He buried his head in his arms and gripped the edges of his bunk with both hands.

"It's not time. It's not time," he screamed.

There were three of them, an officer and two men. The two men stood, for a moment uncertain. The officer slapped him heavily on the shoulder with his open hand. "Take it like a man. It's just as easy," he said good naturedly.

He stopped screaming, but he did not let go, and they had to pull his hands loose and lift him to his feet. He tried to walk down the corridor but his knees were weak and he staggered. The two soldiers, one on either side, supported him.

Outside, it was worse. The pre-dawn air was cold and his thin garments did not turn the damp air of the morning. The dew soaked his shoes. He could not stop shaking. His whole body shook.

"Look at him shiver," the young soldier said. "He'll really quiver in a little while."

"Leave him alone," the older one said. "Don't you see he's doing the best he can?"

As he walked along, his legs got stronger, but his head hurt so badly he felt dizzy. He could not stop the tears that came to his eyes.

"Look, he's crying," the young soldier said.

"It's the wind," he said. "It hurts my eyes."

"It's all right," the older one said. "You're doing fine."

"If it weren't so cold, I'd be all right," he said.

"It's a bad time," the older one said, sympathetically. "You're doing fine. Don't think about it. Just do the best you can."

He felt better then. If only the sun would come up, he would feel better. He would do all right. He would be a man. But when he saw the place, he stopped. His legs would not move and the two soldiers had to support him. His stomach revolted and he gagged emptily.

"What's the matter?" the officer asked, irritated that they had stopped.

"He's sick," the young soldier said, disgusted.

"He doesn't feel good," the older one explained. "He'll be all right in a minute."

"Be a man," the officer said, angrily. "People are watching you."

"I am a man," he whimpered. "I could do as good as any of them if I felt good. I could do as good as you." He began to sob softly.

"Brace up," the officer demanded.

He straightened his back and raised his head, but it was no good.

His legs had turned to water. His head fell to one side and his jaw hung slack. His eyes were empty and far away. Saliva ran down the corner of his mouth and dropped on the young soldier's hand.

The soldier cursed him, and slapped him sharply in the face until he held his head up. He twisted his arm and kicked at his feet to make him stand, but it did no good.

"I'm sick," he wailed, plaintively. "Can't you understand, I'm sick."

"Bring him on," the officer said in disgust. He had done this duty many times.

The two soldiers half-dragged, half-carried him along, grunting under his limp, dead weight. He put his feet down, but his knees buckled under his weight.

"I haven't eaten in two days," he said, apologetically.

"You're doing fine," the older man said. "Don't think about it."

"It wouldn't be so bad if it were light," he said. "A man can face anything in the light. If it were only summer and not so cold."

"We'd all be brave men if the conditions were ideal," the young one said.

"It helps to be ready," the older one said.

descant

"How do you know," he whined piteously.

"I've had to face death many times. It helps if a man is prepared."

They laid him down then, and his breath came irregularly through his mouth with little sucking sounds. He thought he was going to be sick again. The older man held his arms, firmly but gently, talking to him quietly, but he could not hear because he was listening to his own breathing.

"Couldn't you wait until the sun is up?" he asked, his voice shrill in the thin morning air.

"It's a bad time," the older one said gently.

"Give me a few minutes," he pleaded. "Just let me see the sun. It's so cold I can't stand it." His voice trailed off in a scream. He screamed and snarled and tried to bite the older soldier who held him. He screamed a long time, and when he stopped, it took him a while to realize it was not himself screaming now, it was someone else.

The older man was kneeling beside him, talking softly. "It's a big thing," he was saying. "This is a big thing. You want to do your best."

"I can't. I can't," he whimpered. "I'm not ready."

"Then get ready," the young one said, kicking dirt at his face. When he jerked his head away, his arm hurt, and he shrieked involuntarily.

"You've got to get ready," the older one said. "You've got to prepare yourself. Look at that one," he said, nodding his head towards the big one in the middle. "He hasn't made a sound. Now, get yourself ready."

"Not now. Not now," he said.

"Just watch him," the older one said, nodding again at the silent one in the middle.

He watched him. And when they lifted him up and set him in place, the big one spoke. But he could not hear him for his own screams.

Karl Shapiro

What Is Creative Writing?
Or Playing Footsie With the Philistines
—from *descant* 8.3 (Spring 1964)

"Creative writing" is an American expression, like "motel," an invention with which it has much in common. I have never seen the term Creative Writing in a college catalogue, but then I don't read college catalogues. Where I *have* seen it, the name is usually disguised under headings such as "Advanced Composition" or things like that. But the teacher of Creative Writing seldom sees a student who is advanced in composition, and perhaps he would consider such a student a bad risk if he got one. In progressive colleges and a few universities, in expensive private high schools, there may be a Language Arts Department where it really is legal to practice writing poems and novels, but this sort of thing is usually regarded by the authorities as frivolous. For this, nobody in his senses can blame the authorities: to open the educational world to the amateur is a direct threat to education, and only the American educational system has ever opened wide the gates to the Trojan Horse of Creative Writing.

Every person who has ever taught or engaged in a Creative Writing Program has been aware of its absurdity and its essential frivolousness. At the same time, everyone is aware of the necessity of the thing. I have seen terrible battles fought between English departments and Writing departments, battles in which the Trojan Horse is usually destroyed. Nevertheless the writer has become as familiar on the American campus as the modernistic administration building. He is definitely part of the educational landscape.

As I say, this is an American phenomenon. And the American writer can thank his stars that it is. What could he do without the asylum of the university? Where would he go? To that question the answer traditionally has been: Poet, go home (i.e. the waterfront, Bohemia, Skid Row). And of course those places are in many ways

descant

best for the poet, and he will always consider them home sweet home. The American university has taken hundreds of poets off the street. It has been something like a Salvation Army drive. And for recompense the poet has brought something of the color and noise of the street into the hallowed halls. The arrangement has a certain irresponsible gaiety about it. I like it myself.

There is always the danger, of course, that the poet will find himself in a false position as a pseudo scholar. The other day I was one of the examiners for a masters examination on Richardson's *Clarissa*. After about two hours of oral questioning one of my colleagues, a very learned man, remarked casually to the student that he had never read the book. I was so relieved and thunderstruck that I could have thrown my arms around him. I hadn't read it either, but I had read so much about it, by way of cramming for the exam, that I felt thoroughly qualified to question Richardson himself. The poet in the university is not often an educated man: he hasn't had time for it, and he almost always likes books that the rest of the faculty has never even heard of. I have come to the conclusion, after many years of university teaching, that the purpose of a humanities education is to bestow upon the educated man the right to say "I have not read that book." For years I used to lie about books I hadn't read. Being a "professor" has helped me to be honest about such things. More recently I permit myself the luxury of saying I have not read a certain book when I have. The right to say "I have not read that book" is a very precious possession. It belongs to the truly educated man, but the writer comes to it by default. The writer is beyond education, so to speak, and everyone honors, or at least tolerates his ignorance. Until, of course, the writer enters the faculty of a university. Then the fun begins. Even the educated writer, I think, must be something of a thorn in the side of the university. For by definition the writer is always a little ahead of the game; the literary rules have barely been established before he begins to break them (if he is a good writer). And he is not a good writer if he doesn't. The writer who is teaching "Creative" is liable to, and may on purpose, unravel all the student has already learned in the fixed curriculum. Even Archibald MacLeish, a very conservative creative writing teacher, admits that teaching the writing of poetry is the opposite of the academic process. For the subject is not in any book and can never be. The subject is the student himself.

When a new creative writing class assembles in my room I tell them at once: "This is not a class. It is a random collection of people who would like to write. That is the only thing you have in common. You are not in competition with another. There is no competition in art. If you write a genuine poem or story no one will ever be able to duplicate it. No one has had the same experiences; no one, not even your mother, remembers your childhood the way you do. No one will ever share your peculiar angle of vision. Part of your life is going to be lived on paper, maybe the best part, if you are gifted. No one in the world will ever be able to say what you can say." Sometimes I tell them: "Consider yourselves a body of survivors from a sunken ship. Everything is wiped out. There is nothing beyond that horizon. We are completely alone. What good are your books now? Throw them overboard." This frightens a few students; they slip out and run back to the good ship Curriculum.

This sort of talk is not good for most students. It breeds a boyish and piratical attitude towards study. And it encourages the opposite of discipline. Artistic discipline unfortunately is not something that can be taught. What is sauce for the poetic goose may poison the gander. For a long time I used to make everyone learn how to write what is quixotically called iambic pentameter or how to write a sonnet in twenty minutes. But I gave it up as a bad job. Nobody has ever learned anything from copying the *Mona Lisa* except the man who gave her a moustache. Nor is there much point in discussing the theory of forms, plot, structure, and rhetorical figures, if one is going to write. I even insinuate to the class that they had better stay out of philosophy and esthetics rooms; I try to forbid terminology. So it becomes harder and harder to say anything about a poem or story this way, but easier to talk about the people in the thing, easier to valuate the life-quality of the poem.

The hardest task I have with my shipwrecked crew is to make them respect one another. This is your audience, I tell them. Be courteous to them; you may never have another. By courtesy I mean writing in a manner which they can understand. In any given class of any kind there are dull minds and quick ones, but an audience is one mind made up of many. If a piece of writing cannot affect a unity of minds, I consider the work a flop. Of course there is always at least one impatient fellow whose poems are meant only for the teacher. He baits the teacher by going over the heads of the class. If such a lad is actually in advance of the others I usually tell him that I can't help him; that he is already on his own. But he is usually not on his own at all; he is just looking for intellectual companionship. And intellectual companionship he can get elsewhere. Brilliance alone has never made a poet. I have found, in fact, that the brilliant ones seldom make good artists: they are too impatient, and they have as little respect for their fellows as they have for words. It is the oldest cliché in the business and the truth that a writer is a person in love with words. Unfortunately, the most brilliant talkers are usually the seducers rather than the lovers of words. And the man who loves words may be a terrible teacher, a stammerer, and a social oaf. I have never known a poet who did not spill at least one glass of wine on the tablecloth or step on his hostess's foot while he was being introduced.

My students are always skeptical and they laugh when I tell them that they must give up the idea of genius, as another of the falsehoods or misrepresentations of culture. I favor the view, which I call the natural view of art, as against the cultural view, that art is not a matter of individual genius but of the "collectivity." When one studies poetry, say, of the Romantic period, the cultural pinball machine is rolled out. The teacher says "Rousseau" and there is a "ping" and a light lights up. Emerson- "ping" Byron, Shelley, Keats- "ping-ping-ping"-and the game is on. The mechanical assumption is that once upon a time there was a poet of genius who rose from nowhere, or perhaps who rose "from his age"; literary history is never quite sure where he came from and it falls back on the premise that genius (whatever that is) is something rare, unnatural, even freakish. Whereas in my view, genius is the most natural thing in the world. Creativity is the most natural thing in the world. But culture and people who try to keep a tight hand on creativity, taste, value, and the rest, insist on the rarity of art and the man of art. Nothing makes Culture more panicky than a "Renaissance," a time when people at large begin to exercise the natural universal poetic function of creating. It is hard to get this across to the student or to the intimidated public. And because the experts (always self-appointed) are willing to take the responsibility for the Confusion, (Profusion would be a better term) the public gives up natural creativity for the false notion of genius. Let somebody else write my poem, is the defeatist attitude. And someone else usually does. That is where the idea of poet as Spokesman comes in. Yet in any natural, bioculturally healthy world, everybody writes his own poems, even as in a Creative Writing Class.

But are not some of the poems better than others? Are there no standards of comparison? Of course. But the poem is only as good as its audience. A poet who can hold on to his audience century in century out has never existed. A few come close. But that is none of the poet's business, the future, the Classics. I once read that John Ciardi's translation of *The Inferno* had been banned in Pakistan. In the Moslem world *The Divine Comedy* is not a good poem. It is not in my world either. The poem has nothing to say to me. In fact, the historical view of poetry is always the museum view, that every relic is holy and has a bank value. A friend of mine who was a cultural affairs officer in Germany at the close of the Second World War used to tell me about stockpiles of great private libraries and music which the American soldiers had tossed out of windows while looking for cameras and cognac. The barbarians had looted and destroyed, as they had been taught how. The Parthenon was blasted by the Venetians; and the British liberated the Elgin Marbles. All of which is a matter of supreme indifference to the poet, except the phony kind who weeps in the ashes and dreams that every Athens, Ohio, in the world will have a Parthenon. The trouble with every Athens, Ohio, is that it has a Parthenon. There are more Parthenons in Washington, D.C., than there are temples in India. Washington, which architecturally is one of the most depressing and vacuous cities in the world, has never produced a poet or a painter. It is a city of phony Parthenons, in which the creative muse must suffocate. Compare the beauty of Jefferson's University and Monticello with the frightful marble igloo of the Jefferson Memorial.

Nothing is more deadly to creativity than Standards. And to the writer who wanders into my class I say: you are the standard. Certainly

I tell them things to read, but I tell each one a different story. As a group I try to unburden them of the weight of opinion and prejudice of literary name-dropping. This process has nothing to do with education; it has to do with non-education. Education (I am speaking of humanistic education) is an end in itself, and insofar as I know the end, I revere it. But education, unfortunately, has little or nothing to do with creating poems. Education tells us: "This is how it happened." Poetry says: "Maybe it did, but I don't see it that way." And the poet starts rewriting the history book. What is missing in education generally is the life quality of the works. Culture is always horrified by any sign of life. A "genius" is an artist who somehow escaped the culture police. In the career of every writer there is always the lifelong battle against cultural authority. The authorities try to preserve the standards of the past against the life-urge of the present. Culture authority is eternally against the present, eternally despises the present. But the poet says: this is the only life I know.

And in our country too the battle of the poet against culture authority goes on. It is poet against literature, poet against the past, against tradition. By nature the poet is not against anything, but by nature he demands the keys to the present. In America we still have a basically healthy situation in which we encourage the poet, the artist, the composer, etc. to come up and speak. Highbrow culture does everything in its power to destroy this natural creativity but it has not succeeded, and I do not think it will.

From a broad point of view in America right now, there are three kinds of writing: (1) "Creative" Writing (2) Books and (3) Literature. These divisions need no explanation. Creative Writing is new untried literature. Book manufacture is book business. And Literature is "lasting books."

The categories are somewhat complicated by the facts that Lasting Books can be Business (Literature Business) and that Creative Writing helps stoke the furnace of the publishers and to spread a fine literary ash throughout the cultural atmosphere. But in America book business is not big business; it is middlesize business. Publishers, as far as I know, are not listed on the Stock Exchange along with motor cars and fat cattle. On the other hand, the magazine business is definitely

Big. Some comic books, I am told, sell as many as fifty million copies a week, and the Luce magazines are almost in the same bracket. The Luce magazines are of course literary, in the sense that they dictate values. There is no cultural need of modern man that is not taken care of by the anonymous authors of these weekly journals, including poetry and other branches of Creative Writing. If we were asked what is the most weighty authority for literature in America today, we would have to answer in all seriousness, not T. S. Eliot, not the American University or the public library, neither some famous writer nor the Tradition: the literary authority in America today is *Time* magazine. And that is a loathsome thought.

I want to comment on the three kinds of writing I have mentioned in this manner. Literature first, Book Manufacturing second, and Creative Writing third. But first a word about tripartite cultural habits:

I have often noticed that intellectuals are people who count up to three and then stop. The 20th century tri-istic formula comes from the old Thesis-Antithesis-Synthesis, translated culturally into Mass Culture, Middle Class Culture, and High Culture. In a recent book by Dwight Macdonald, a professional intellectual, he reduces these counters to Masscult, Midcult, and (so far by implication) Hicult. Masscult is to him the enemy; Midcult a contamination from below, and Hicult, of course, what is approved of by the intellectuals, and by the Luce magazines, which Macdonald helped organize. The terms are phony but all intellectuals use them in one form or another. But they do not describe any reality.

In any case, Hicult stands for "Literature." Literature is supposedly the real thing. Literature is the standard for the highbrow writer, as it is, for better reasons, in the college curriculum. Literature is an anchor. It is sunken treasure and salvage. It is always being dredged up and sold, or put in museums. You will almost never find a new or an unknown poet in these magazines. Literature means a standstill, a freeze. The entire idea of Literature is to prevent change, to keep up the museum. The museum is a combination of a prison, a school, a hospital, and a bank. No artist ever painted a picture for a museum; no poet ever wrote a poem for an anthology. Yet Literature always ends up in the Anthology. Paintings end up behind bars, with the art gallery guard wearing a pistol on his hip. The poor artist, we are always told, died of starvation, but his paintings were sold for millions after the funeral. What is the meaning of this? The meaning is that the intellectuals have cornered the market, literally, for critical speculation, authority and reward.

The aim of Literature, with a capital L, is to suppress literature. The aim of Literature is to kill itself off. It does very well at this enterprise but it never quite succeeds. New Literature is always popping up, new weeds that can't be weeded out. Then somebody one day decrees that a certain weed is really a flower. The Literary Stock Market goes into secret session and decides that a certain ragweed (say, Mark Twain) is really a sweet-smelling blossom of Literature. Whereupon Mark Twain is raised to the stature of Henry James. Macdonald, a true-blue intellectual, is very suspicious of Mark Twain because Mark Twain reaches "the common people." In dialectical fashion, he divides Clemens into two people. Macdonald, who is bothered about Mark Twain's greatness as a writer and his popularity, says that Mark Twain had a real Literary life and a low-cult comedian kind of life. He can't see that the two things are really one and the same thing.

What Hicultists are constitutionally incapable of understanding is that the writer doesn't believe in the class structure of Literature. And that, when the real writer, Mark Twain or Whitman or Shakespeare gladly runs down instead of UP he is not running to perdition but to his audience. This is why the greatest writers usually have a powerful sense of comedy and absurdity and—a word I like—hilarity.

And even though all Classic literature is infused with comic works, no Literature man ever deigns to recognize contemporary comedy. The reason is that contemporary comedy is always "Mass Cult." Literature cannot tolerate Mass-cult; it cannot tolerate any manifestation of life. It must set warning signs, buoys, guideposts, fiats, thou-shalt-nots. It hates what it calls mass-communications; it hates crowds, groups, and audiences. Especially audiences. Under Literature the Audience shrinks to a family, to a one-man operation. While down below there is always a rumble of laughter. In the comic expression:

the natives are restless tonight. The natives are always restless. That is why they are natives.

Literature is standardization at the top. It has no other business than to fix standards and to set burglar alarms. Macdonald says in his attacks on Masscult and Midcult that only the Little Magazines (highbrow journals) today care about standards. He is right, and that is what is wrong with the Little Magazine. Standards of course are always exclusive and authoritarian in literature. Throughout Literature the purveyors of Standards have acted as the brake upon the natural creativity of man. The culture academy has invariably resisted the life impulse in the arts. Recently it took an act of the French Chamber of Deputies to open up some of the vaults of the Louvre to permit a few buried pictures to be shown. It will take a fullscale critical revolution in this country to regain a place for Walt Whitman. Every highbrow journal in America is today in a state of hysteria because the spread of Beat poetry, fiction, and jazz, and the worldwide manifestations of revolt against standards. One need not be a defender of the Beat to recognize that it is or was another of the age-old upheavals against fixed and traditional standards.

I do not think we should flatter ourselves with the old pedagogical flattery that culture swings back and forth in some kind of Classical-Romantic pendulum, that we have first a Romantic movement of the clock and then a Classical respite, and so on. Every revolt against standards and standard-fixing is, rather, a step forward in man's struggle for ultimate and final freedom. The conditions of cultural control must eventually and finally give way before the universal human urge to create. The superstition of genius will become as obsolete as the coat of mail; the cult of personality will be forgotten. The world of critics, estheticians, and art experts is still reeling from the gigantic creative earthquakes of the Renaissance; yet the Renaissance was no more than an earth-tremor in man's awakening consciousness, compared to what is to come. The curators of Standards shudder to think of another such humanistic eruption; hence their bitter opposition to normal, amateur creativity, their frantic defenses of Literature and the Classics, their hatred of simplicity and their worship of the secret and hieratic art form. The highbrow's terror of Masscult or

descant

Midcult is a pure terror of life; the Hicultist's worship of death even extends to a ghoulish belief in the dead artist, the suicide, the pathological freak as the only artist worth talking about. After death the pictures go on sale; after death Hopkins is discovered; Emily Dickinson is discovered, Mozart is discovered. And woe to the artist who is popular in his lifetime, whether Burns or Shakespeare. The Bureau of Standards won't give him a passing grade.

In the biologic process of poetry all things are possible. Literature is indeed beautiful, the artificial paradise of history, yet it is always more dead than alive. Natural creative man has always been ostracized from the Garden of Literature; yet he is taught to yearn for it as a kind of heaven. But whoever enters this garden knows it for what it is, the cemetery of poetry. And outside, where we are, man is taught to be ashamed of poetry; taught that only genius is capable of art and that genius happens only once in a blue moon. I used as the motto of my book of collected essays the words "everything we are taught is false." It is a saying of Rimbaud's: I apply it to Literature.

Natural artistic creation belongs to the whole of mankind. Think of the Gothic cathedrals, none of which is tagged with the name of the artist. And think, on the other hand, of the Cathedral of Barcelona, a modern work which George Orwell regretted was not blown up by the anarchists during the Spanish Civil War. The Barcelona monstrosity is of course a great favorite among art critics and other experts. Compare the eruption of European poetry during the Renaissance with the shrinking of poetry in the 20th century. Compare the universality of Hindu sculpture, painting, and building for more than two thousand years with the absolute death of all the arts in India, dating from the time of the Western cultural invasion, largely under the direction of Lord Cornwallis, whose previous assignment was at Yorktown. When India became independent in 1950 the art of dancing (one of the greatest in the world, as we know from the sculptures) had disappeared so completely that one person (an Englishwoman) single-handedly tried to revive it by traveling through the jungles to find old people who still remembered something about it. There were no sculptors left, in a vast country which is almost literally carved in stone from one end to the other. There is today only one painter in India, Jamini Roy, in a land that created the anonymous masterpieces of Ajanta and Elura. Think, finally, of the dramatic collapse of the Noh drama in Japan, at the very moment of entry of Commodore Perry. As in India, the Noh play had to be revived from the memory of old men who remembered it fifty years later.

History, which invariably reaps the whirlwind, destroys the biologic creativity of the human race. Yet as long as the human race exists, universal art springs up under our feet. Does history destroy art intentionally as it destroys man himself? I don't know. The historical consciousness is always death to natural art; I believe this is true. The biologic creativity of man flourishes only when the historical consciousness dies. The more history the less art. Think of Soviet Russia, a nation bent upon historical determinism (as they call it), a nation dedicated to some superstition of the Historical Process. Look at their art. There is none. It is against the law. Contemporary Russian architecture, say the University of Moscow, is probably at the lowest point ever reached in the history of architecture. The painting is almost unbelievably lifeless. The literature we know about. What Russian poets did not kill themselves or were not killed, walked proudly into silence. The emergence of two Russian poets in the past several years is a triumph of human creativity over political destructiveness—but the Kremlin keeps a close watch on what in Russia is probably called those biological throwbacks—Evtushenko and Voznesbevsby. Only the musician barely escaped. I believe that the great release of dramatic poetry in Elizabethan times was a release from history, from the tyranny of the Church, and from the tyranny of the European historical process. I can never believe that man is a creature of history. Man comes to life when history has a fainting spell.

According to my view, which reverses the standard hierarchy of values, things get better as you go down and worse as you go up. Hicult to me signifies the death of natural creativity. Midcult is healthier, though contaminated by Hicult; and Masscult is the real thing, or close to it. In reality we have no healthy mass art or literature because it is prohibited or sabotaged by Hicult.

Book Manufacture shares the characteristics of both Hicult and

Locult. In the publishing business the Hicult writer is always used as a standard, for purposes of advertising. For instance, if a young man publishes a novel and it has the imprimatur of, say, Faulkner or Gide, or Henry James, or just a blurb, it is at once introduced to Literary High Society. At the same time, if a book is a best-seller, it attracts the suspicious attention of Hicult. Book Business really is in the middle; it can never impress Hicult and can never touch bottom, where the creativity comes from. All the same, it uses the divining rod of literary instinct to locate the sources of power and fertility; and now and then it succeeds where Hicult fails. Hicult is happier in tight little cultures, such as big cities which operate a monopoly of the means of book production and museums. The big publishers are always in big cities, where the Hicultists hang out to control the literary stock market. When a literary monopoly shifts its base, or defection becomes evident, the literary stock market panics. A recent example is the defection of Bohemia from New York to San Francisco. The terrifying thing to Hicult is that the Bohemia has its own organs of publication. This knocks the bottom out from Hicult, which tries to regulate publication and sometimes succeeds by claiming a monopoly for their so-called Little Magazine. The Little Magazine has long been propagandized as a saintly and penniless literary venture, without which no first-rate writer would ever be published. This is partly the case. But The Little Magazine is not of course content to be little. Mr. Macdonald tells how he tried to convince Henry Luce to start a culture magazine to put the icing on the cake of *Time, Life, Fortune,* and *Sport*. As Hicultist, Macdonald was trying to tie up American culture in a Masscult magazine. But Mr. Luce *already* had it tied up in his other magazines. Eventually he may move in and bootleg wholesale culture, in the same way that he now bootlegs theology, ethics, politics, medicine, business, painting, baseball, education, and crime.

    I am not convinced that the industry of books in this country is an evil. At least ninety percent of the books in America every year *are* a dead loss and a waste, and yet I think it is better to overproduce books than to put creativity into quarantine. The appalling badness of the majority of books, whether poetry, fiction, or what librarians ironically call "non-fiction" is, it seems to me, a condition of nature. We do books on a trial and error basis; the book man gambles on them and usually loses. And books become the raw material for movies and television, radio and all the other things that horrify Hicult. Yet inferior books disappear like weeds or dead foliage; undoubtedly they have an enriching quality like guano. The common literary fare may disgust the literateur *but it is the bridge to true creativity,* which exists in the mass, universally. Book Business is necessarily tentative but it is the only available thoroughfare to mass creativity. Even a Hicult work of art of any kind is eventually decided upon by the sub-literary mass, and rightly so. Any other form of decision is personal, dictatorial, and arbitrary. The 20th century example of this kind of literary arbiter is T. S. Eliot, who is supported by all the Hicultist magazines and by Henry Luce, who works on the same principle in journalism. I call it the Starvation Principle of Art.

Book Business supports poetry weakly. Poetry has been in a state of psychic shock for centuries (in the white world), a juicy fact upon which T. S. Eliot and other art dictators have founded their fortunes. As poetry is the most natural, common, universal art, the prototype of arts, its sickness invites quackery of every sort. In America there is no natural poetry; or rather, the natural poetry is diverted into other channels: fiction, comedy, advertising, and even business. Book Manufacturing is well aware that poetry has no audience; it supports a token poetic element partly out of nostalgia, partly out of guilt, mostly out of cynicism and fear of Hicult. There is a broader base, nevertheless, for poetry in Book Business than there is among the Hicultists. The Hicultist can barely assimilate one new poet in a generation; usually he is two or three generations behind even his own new "Discoveries." Every anthology is a country club or an Academy to which a new member is admitted only when another member is dead. Thus the principle of the Academy, as we all know; limited membership, more or less hereditary, with an annual lecture on cultural taxidermy, attended by all the reigning dodos.

Book Business is a prisoner of the cultural situation. And the Cultural Situation is always the artificial paradise from which man is excluded. I can't think of a more thankless occupation than book publishing in the United States. Americans don't worship books (and

descant

you can't blame them). When I was in the army I invariably heard soldiers refer to magazines and comic books and books themselves all as books. To an American a magazine is a book. If anyone thinks this is an unintentional or illiterate error I beg to differ. We have the healthiest contempt for books of any people in the world.

The Book Business finally got around to publishing books in paper covers. Overnight a volume of anything that never sold more than 300 copies, began to sell half a million. Not because of price. People started to buy books because they looked a little more like magazines. That is the meaning of the book to the soldier, the throwaway, not the precious volume that needs a niche in the living room. The book after all is only a magazine undergoing rigor mortis. Or it is a thing to learn by rote, a schoolbook. Or it is a holy book to put in the drawer of a hotel room. It is never anything that can be passed from hand to hand for pleasure. The paperbook in America probably started during the Second World War for overseas troops. Paper volumes of everything from the classics to bedroom novels not yet released were printed in editions of over a hundred thousand per book. No one was permitted to bring one of these subversive paperbacks home. Book Business and Army Regulations forbade these little editions from returning to the U.S. They are today collector's items. The Library of Congress has one of the few complete collections. But every soldier read books in the little throwaway form. And after that War the Book Business got the message. What I am saying is that this delayed reaction was not a matter of book economics but of cultural control from the top, the Hicult's shibboleth that people don't like to read.

There is no question that there are more books published today in the United States in one year than in the whole of the rest of the world for every century since the printing of the Gutenberg Bible.

The publishing business in America is the Hyde Park or Bughouse Square of our country. But instead of confining our crackpots to a parked-in area, quietly surrounded by police, we have them print their immortal works. There is probably more freedom of book-printing in America today than in any other country. I don't know about freedom of the press. The press is hamstrung by big business and politics. The newspaper is not as free in America as the book. Book-wise, we are back in the era of Tom Paine, destroying literary institutions right and left. Newspaper-wise, we are probably in the era of Napoleon III or something. And there is no good literary newspaper in the U.S., no really reliable one. *The New York Times*, which is famous for its encyclopedic thoroughness, is weakest in literary matters. All American writers complain from time to time of the absence of literary news or rational literary criticism in the U.S. So-called liberal papers like *The Nation* and *The New Republic* are more reactionary than liberal in literature, more theoretical than practical. During the last newspaper strike in New York a group of writers founded a newspaper for reviewing books—the best of its kind yet to come along. Yet it is unique in this country and probably will not survive. For one thing it is definitely colored by Hicultism. But now and then I receive weird and fantastic papers in mimeograph style, which leap from homeprinting to bookform; that is, make the leap from free speech to Literature overnight. This was the case with the so-called obscene poem "Howl," which in a matter of months sped from "unprintable" bookstore pamphlet to anthology, even through the barrier of a nationally-advertised court case, in which professors from the University of California defended the poem and won the court decision. This points not so much to chaos as to old-fashioned self-expression. Freedom of expression by definition is a mass prerogative. In a controlled cultural situation, such as exists in every part of Europe and in Hicult America, book production is always limited, screened from the top. I am convinced that the whole superstition of the Literary Movement which we read about in histories, is a matter of literary politics. Recall that for centuries it was illegal for anyone to publish anything without somebody or other's permission; that it is only recently that a woman could become a writer and not be considered a monster. Even though publishing in this country is conservative and unimaginative, it provides the only gateway to what Macdonald calls Masscult, and what I call natural creativity.

    The gauche term "creative writing" signifies that something is wrong with writing. If we have creative writing there must then be uncreative writing. And indeed there is uncreative writing. People also make a distinction between poets and "writers," even though poet is a generic term meaning creative writer. Every writer who deserves the name is a poet, whether he writes fiction, philosophy, history, or verse, or anything else. But the word poet has in the rational age been split away from "writer," leaving the vulgar image of the poet as dreamer or idealist. A brain-washed Buddha. In my own experience I have never met a poet who was either a dreamer or an idealist. Realist or hypnotist would be more like it.

Creative writing as a discipline in America points to the fact that poetry is not yet natural in America and that it survives as a criticism of "writing."

It sounds unpleasant to say that poetry is unnatural in America. And it sounds even odder that we teach the writing of poetry. Shakespeare didn't study creative writing, nor did Milton or Sophocles. Frequently when students come to me to enter a poetry class (creative writing) I ask them why they want to write poetry; and very often they reply: my father is a business man or an engineer or a doctor, and I don't want to be any of those things. In other words, they don't want to sacrifice the joy of life to social respectability or economic security alone. Theirs is a good reply. Most of my young writers will try to enter the teaching profession, as the most decent, though least remunerative, of the professions. The American University, as everyone knows, has become an asylum for artists of all kinds. It has become the only cultural community in the United States that makes sense. But it is a temporary asylum for the creative. Sooner or later the poet or artist must make his way back to the world and take his rightful place as a creator, alongside the merchant, the lawyer, and the bridge-builder. But the artist is still pocketed up in America in skidrows, or protected in the colleges and universities, which more and more recognize his value. The poet is generally a restless guest in the university but at least he knows he is welcome. There is no welcome for him elsewhere.

Hicult has always thrived on Left-Bankism, exploiting the Artist as a so-called enemy of society. But the true artist is neither for nor against society. Hicult becomes enraged when the artist refuses the bribes of cultural authority and it then turns on the artist in skidrow and joins with the police in trying to exterminate him. The attacks on Beat Existentialist and "absurd" writers come from both the police and from Hicultists such as Macdonald. Hicult has once again made Bohemia a word of opprobrium and once again has postponed the natural communication of the poet with the rest of the community. The always poetry-starved middle, the majority of modern men everywhere, remains isolated from Hicult and Low, and continues to fidget with the TV set or whatever new gadget has come along. The explosive creative energies of the middle classes in America, which are denied true creative outlets at the top and bottom, turn to fantastic machine constructions, business, violent sports, politics, and war. The terminology and iconography of American progress and science are always couched in the language of war: the conquest of space or of Mt. Everest, the *struggle* against nature and disease, the *fight* against poverty, and so on. American creativity is always diverted into byways called Progress, almost never into natural creativity. Even our arts are used as weapons in a so-called propaganda war; Culture becomes a battle-cry. When this happens, the natural poet withdraws further and further from the cultural scene or he becomes nihilistic.

Hicult is in terror of natural art. Macdonald even complains of the popularity of jazz, preferring the closed audience of the Newport Jazz Festival. The Hibrow aristocracy even tries to prevent jazz from reaching its natural audience, which is world-wide. Riots occurred at one of the Newport Jazz Festivals a few years back which the newspapers represented as Beatnik gangs. They were merely people who wanted to hear the music. Jazz is the one natural art America has contributed to the world. It was despised from its inception by Hicult (with T. S. Eliot sneering at the saxophone and the jazz form), but it is now claimed as something interesting after all for the intellectual. A bit late, however; jazz escaped the clutches of Hicult generations ago.

Now Hicult opposes "jazz poetry" poetry for performance or whatever the names it goes under. To Hicult, poetry is something you study on the page, under the magnifying glass, after a good European education. To make poetry go to music, or even say it out loud, is a crime to the ears of Hicult. If you say it out loud somebody might hear it; worse, they might like it; there is even the horrible probability that any Tom, Dick, and Harry will begin to write the stuff. Hence the Hicult sneers at Creative Writing, Writers Conferences, and other manifestations of interest in natural poetry, music, or painting.

Creative Writing, of course, is no solution to anything. It is merely a sign that the cultural police haven't locked all the doors.

In this country where poetry has never taken root, a little hierarchy still rules the literary roost. About six literary quarterlies, if that many, make all the decisions about poetry, as far as respectability goes. These decisions are purveyed to a non-existent mass public through one or two slick news magazines, like *Time*. *Time* will on occasion try to run the whole show, as on at least one occasion when they tried to award the Pulitzer Prize to one of their staff. The maneuver failed, but they gave it a go. There is definitely a liaison between Hicult and *Time*, about as unholy an alliance as I can think of. But the public won't buy it, won't buy either the high-powered small-circulation culture quarterly or the culture opinion of the slick news magazines.

Some of you may have read an article by Archibald MacLeish about the teaching of creative writing. In it he says many fine things and he says them well, and yet he ends up defending traditional culture against (using the most pressing example) the San Francisco skidrow poetry and music. He even tries to present the university as a center of gaiety and life. The defense is accurate to a certain extent: the university has become a preserve of culture in America, much as it was in the Middle Ages, because outside the university there are marauding gangs of jesuitical intellectuals ready to place on the rack any dissenter from holy Hicult writ. "If we are to judge by its works (says MacLeish) there can scarcely be a worse place to get admitted to life than San Francisco." I think MacLeish makes the classic mistake when he refuses to accept vitality at the bottom. The escape from New York and New England is something which offends him, as it does all the guardians of Culture. And I would suppose that the greatest disappointment of the recent Bohemian upsurge is that it is now exploited by tourism, *Time* magazine, and even Madison Avenue. Which only goes to prove that the Bottom is never deep enough, that poetry is always plucked up by the roots before it has a chance to bud. All the artist ever asks of the world is to be left alone; and that is precisely what the world of culture and progress will never do. A person from Porlock is always at the door, whether the Collection Agency, the Literary Critic, or the Nobel Prize Committee. Culture is more persistent than a Baptist missionary. It invades the jungle of Creativity even before the businessman arrives with his oil drills and his hospitals. And its antiseptics are permanent. Every artist knows this as the first fact of life. He runs from Left Bank to Left Bank forever, in a comedy of escape which the literateur ponderously and hypocritically calls "Exile."

Poetry and all creativity will perhaps become natural in this country for the first time and at long last, because of the ultimate rout of Hicult and everything it stands for. The poet will shortly accept Masscult as his natural medium and in whatever form it takes, T.V., Broadway, the films, advertising, journalism, comic book, Beat manifesto, or *Playboy*. Everything at the bottom, and everything in the mass belongs to the artist. It is his medium and his birthright. It seems to me that poetry is about to be born in our country. Hicult is finally on the run; the Standard-makers are facing moral and intellectual bankruptcy; the Little Magazine has defected from the Headquarters of Culture and is fraternizing with the Enemy; the book is once again a magazine; poetry has left the laboratory for the nightclub and the coffee house, the theatre and the opera stage. And modern poetry is happily, triumphantly dead.

All of the arts everywhere in the world today where creativity is alive are engaging in what they call in one form or another "Pure drama. Anti-Thematic, anti-ideological, anti-social-realist, anti-philosophical, anti-boulevard psychology, anti-bourgeois . . ." It is not negation—unless it be the negation of the permanent, of the criterion of the headstone. It is by questioning the old truths to death that our century has produced such riches in every realm of creativity. But we have only made a beginning. The French dramatist Eugene Ionesco hits the nail on the head when he says: "Back to the unendurable! *Back to dislocation!* Disarticulation of language too! As for poetry, as for any literary art, now it is time to make words say things they never meant."

Art today stands face to face with Masscult and has no choice but to merge with it.

Robert Penn Warren

Learning to Write
—from *descant* 9.3 (Spring 1965)

The topic on which I am going to talk this morning is scarcely a new one. But I am not going to apologize for that. I certainly am not going to apologize to a group of writers for not introducing a new topic, for writers know, or ought to know, better than anybody else that the old topics are always best. Boy gets girl. How beautiful is the sunset. Love *vs.* honor. Right and wrong. To be or not to be. Writers ought to know that topics, that ideas, are nothing. That is, are nothing in themselves, as abstractions. But they also know—or rather, they are engaged in the constant effort to know—that ideas operative are everything. But I am not about to say that I hope to make my old topic, my old idea, operative. That is up to you, as writers. For ideas only become operative in art. Or in action. Which is the same thing, for in these terms, at this level, in reference to ideas, art and action are interchangeable. Both art and action are concerned with the idea formative and not the idea formed.

But to define my topic: Can writing be learned?

Right away, I shall say that, in one sense, the answer is no. By this no, however, I don't mean the easy dodge which relieves us of all responsibility and flatters each of us in his secret soul: the poet is born, not made. I mean something like this, instead: No artist can ever say, "Now I have learned to write, and I think I'll start tomorrow morning." One thing that distinguishes the art from the craft is the fact that the art is never learned. A cabinet-maker learns to make a cabinet and a shoe-maker learns to make a shoe, and having learned his craft he can make innumerable cabinets and innumerable shoes. But a painter never learns to paint a picture; he only learns certain things which he can use in the process of learning to paint a particular picture, and he doesn't learn to paint that picture until he has painted it, has finished the job. When he gets ready to paint the next picture—in so far as he is artist and not craftsman—he has to start all over again. True, he starts with richer resources and with keener sensibilities, but he has a new problem of exploration on his hands. He has to learn a new solution, and the new solution is the new picture. The word *new* is the important word here. If the picture is not new, really new, the painter is not an artist, he is merely a copyist, merely a craftsman copying himself. But we shall come back to this matter of exploration, and shall probably end there.

Meanwhile, let us take a fresh start toward that end, and let us invoke a sacred name: In the *Meno* we find the question, "Can virtue be taught?" At one stage in the argument, Meno himself puts the following objection to Socrates: "How will you enquire, Socrates, into that which you do not know?" And Socrates restates the objection in the form of a paradox: "You argue that a man cannot enquire either about that which he knows, or about that which he does not know; for if he knows, he has no need to enquire; and if not, he cannot; for he does not know the very subject about which he is to enquire." Socrates goes on to a refutation of this sophistical objection, but we may re-cast it into the terms of our own topic: can writing be learned? If a man has already written what he wants to write, he has no need to learn how to write that thing; and if he does not know what he wants to write, he does not know the very subject about which he is trying to learn. Now we recognize that this is sophistical, too, ultimately. But perhaps at a level a little less than ultimate, it has some sense to it, the kind of sense which prompted the following remark which was made to me several years ago by a distinguished American novelist who had been lured into doing a hitch in the academic grove. He said: "I can't teach these people how to write. Not really. All I can do is to teach them how to write novels exactly like my novels, and even if my novels are any good, these people, if they are any good, don't want to learn to write novels like my novels." He was simply restating the same paradox.

Something inside us tells us that this paradox can be resolved. But it may be worth our while to glance at the terms in which often during the past centuries it has been resolved, or rather, evaded. It can be evaded by either of two time-honored views of the nature of art and of artistic tradition. It is tempting to use as labels for these views the words *classic* and *romantic*, but to do so would do wrong to writers who also bear those labels in our text books. It would do them wrong, for, I believe, no real artist ever held, in his function as artist, either of these as yet unlabelled views; he may have deluded himself into saying that he held one or the other, but we, looking at his work, can always know better. I wouldn't worry about doing the critics wrong on this score, for too many of them have done themselves wrong, and quite publicly, on this score. But, for convenience, we shall have to give some sort of label, and I shall quite arbitrarily call one view the "bag of tricks" view and the other the "letting-down-the-back-hair" view.

We are familiar with both views, for they are flung around irresponsibly in the Sunday literary supplements and in the weekly reviews and, alas, in the books reviewed in the reviews. And we fling them around, too, at our convenience, on the old principle that any stick is good enough to beat a dog—the dog always being some book which we don't like or a book by somebody whom we don't like.

The first view, the "bag-of-tricks" view, says that art is purely and simply technique, that there are certain fixed ways of doing things "right," that there are certain ideal forms for the various types—for the short story, the novel, the lyric, the epic, the tragedy, the comedy, the pastoral, the elegy, and all the other categories Polonius might list.

According to this view, the art can be learned quite simply and directly as you would learn to make the cabinet or the cake. Once you have the "rule" you can settle down to the business of production. There will be, of course, some incidental difficulties—the wood may have a knot in it, or the grain won't take the varnish well, or there is a tendency to split when you sink the nail. But if the wood is too bad, you can throw it away and simply pick up another piece that can be worked according to the rule.

This is an old conception—the rule of making. "Art is methodical efficiency" the Middle Ages said, quoting a Latin rhetorician. And the Middle Ages didn't make the distinction, dear to our modern hearts,

descant

between fine arts and useful arts; painters might be classed with saddle-makers (because saddles were painted) and sculptors would be classed with stone-cutters and masons. And even as late as the sixteenth century we find Leonardo making a peculiar distinction, which offends against our notion of the fine arts, between painting and sculpture on the grounds that a painter could wear fine clothes like a gentleman and not get mussed while a sculptor had to dress like a workman. And the Middle Ages, again, often classed poetry as a subdivision of rhetoric or logic or grammar.

But this notion didn't go out with the Middle Ages. Poetry remained, for many commentators, an appendage of logic or rhetoric—art in so far as it could be reduced to rule—and we can run across statements that poetry differs from ordinary logic only in so far as it uses the syllogism of example instead of the syllogism of demonstration. This whole idea of literature as something that could be reduced to the rule and therefore learned directly received, as a matter of fact, an enormous support from the worship of the classics in the Renaissance, and from the resulting doctrine of imitation. The great past had set the supreme examples, and the business of the present was simply to study the rules whereby the result had been achieved, and then go and do likewise. And we get the extreme case in the cult of Ciceronianism, which would limit itself to the very vocabulary and phrases used by the model.

When we come across these notions they always strike us with some surprise, for we remember the actual literary works of the age and not the critics, and we know that, despite what the critics said, the works themselves aren't very much like the advertised models but were new—*The Faerie Queene* and *Hamlet* and *Paradise Lost*. The artists—the real artists—knew better than the rule-makers, the critics, and went right on busily learning in their own way. And I suppose that Petrarch put the matter as well as anybody when he said that the resemblance between the modern work and the ancient model should be that of son to father and not that of portrait to sitter.

We nod approvingly at Petrarch's remark and sniff at the rule-makers, but unhappily we haven't always attained to Petrarch's wisdom or outgrown the rule-makers for whom literature is a craft of forms. Every age sets up its own rules and screams bloody murder when somebody starts tampering with them. They screamed bloody murder at Keats and they screamed bloody murder at Wordsworth and then another generation or two later they screamed bloody murder at people who didn't want to look like more Wordsworth or Keats. They screamed bloody murder at Browning and at Zola and at Ibsen and at Hardy and at Proust and at Eliot and at Joyce. And now you occasionally hear a scream of bloody murder directed at somebody because he doesn't resemble Proust or Eliot or Joyce. I don't mean to imply that the new is always good, but I do mean to say that the doctrine of abstract forms is always bad and that it is always with us. Thomas Jefferson said that a government needs a revolution every twenty years; and so does the Republic of Letters. And it almost always gets one, even if not every twenty years. Proust said that it takes fifty years for a new artistic idiom to become established and Frau Ibsen said that her husband didn't expect one of his works to be understood in less than ten years; but whatever the time required, it does take some time to win the battle against the rule-makers, and then the generation which won the battle against the rule-makers wants to make up its own rules and fight, bleed, and die for them. And brooding over the scene of carnage, there is always some sad, benign, aloof, professorial face from the lips of which fall the words, "Shakespeare is good enough for me." Alas the trouble is not that Shakespeare is not good enough for us but that he is too good for us. And too good, too, for the gentleman with the sad, benign face. Shakespeare solved his problems better than we can hope to solve ours, but we have ours to solve, and he will never help us to solve them if we read him by rule and not by principle.

So much for the "bag-of-tricks" view.

But let us turn to the "let-down-the-back-hair" view. Just as the "bag-of-tricks" view says that writing—or any art—can be learned simply and directly according to rule—by the mastery of the forms abstractly considered—so the "let-down-the-back-hair" view says that it can't be learned, that it is the result of inspiration pure and simple. This view, too, has a long history. If we open any anthology of criticism, or any history of criticism, we find the following passage on the first page, or thereabouts: "For all the epic poets, the good ones, utter all their beautiful poems not through art but because they are divinely inspired and possessed, and the same is true of the good lyric poets. For just as the Corybantes are not in their right minds, so the lyric poets are not in their right minds when they compose their beautiful poems, but when they enter into harmony and rhythm they revel as though they were possessed, like the Bacchae who when they are possessed draw honey and milk from the rivers but cannot do so when in their right minds ... the craft of the poet is light and winged and holy, and he is not capable of poetry until he is inspired by the gods and out of his mind and there is no reason in him." And for thousands of years we find the poets invoking the muses or the gods. And a couple of thousand of years after the composition of the above passage, we find such testimony as this from Mozart: "My ideas come as they will, I don't know how, all in a stream. If I like them, I keep them in my head, and people say that I often hum them over to myself. Well, if I can hold on to them, they begin to join on to one another, as if they were bits that a pastry-cook should join together in his pantry. And now my soul gets heated, and if nothing disturbs me the piece grows larger and larger and brighter until, however long it is, it is all finished together in my mind, so that I can see it at a glance, as if it were a pretty picture or a pleasing person. Then I don't hear the notes one after another, as they are hereafter to be played, but it is as if in my fancy there they were all at once. And that is a revel. While I'm inventing it all seems to be like a fine vivid dream; but that hearing it all at once (when the invention is done), that's the best. What I have once so heard I forget not again, and perhaps this is the best gift that God has granted me" (quoted by Josiah Royce, *The Spirit of Modern Philosophy*, p. 457). And Wordsworth talked about the spontaneous overflow of powerful feelings, and Shelley, who in poetry could ask the wind to make him its lyre even as the forest was, could, in sober prose, speak of the soul in the process of creation glowing like a coal under the fitful gusts of imagination—or something of the sort. And we remember how old Caedmon, ashamed because he could not sing, retired to the stables where he heard the voice say, "Caedmon, sing." And we remember how all Coleridge had to do to get a particularly beautiful poem was to drowse off and dream it through to the point where the vulgar person from Porlock knocked on the door and scared the muse out the window. We know, for instance, that Shakespeare left scarcely a blot on his papers. And these descriptions and examples of the inspired moment could be multiplied indefinitely.

We like to dwell on them because they tell us what we already know to be true—that artistic creation is a miracle. We know that all these happy witnesses are telling the truth about their own experiences, too. But what are we to make of this "truth"?

Well, we know what people sometimes make of it. They make of it that to get the poem or the novel or the play you just spill your innards on the table, and the result is bound to be fascinating because so true, oh, so true. They make of it that good writing is a fine burst of feeling, a delicious emotional blur, a great shiny froth like white of egg under an electric beater, a holy intoxication and not "one halfpennyworth of bread to this intolerable deal of sack!" They make of it that if you want to write you just keep paper and pencil handy and wait until that spark from heaven falls or the Muse finally works around to your address like the census-taker. And when the happy moment comes, for goodness sake, don't have any second thoughts about what you put on paper, or—God forbid!—any third thoughts, for poetry must be simple, sensuous, and passionate.

This view has some interesting manifestations, or perhaps corollaries. We have, for instance, a peculiar distortion of expressionistic aesthetics which amounts to the notion that all you have to do to get a masterpiece is simply to express the "self" in its purity—whatever that means. Whatever it means positively, it means negatively that you don't have to bother about the nature of your medium or your materials—you simply slam on the paint or slam down the words, and it is bound to come out right, because it is you, you, you. Or we have the notion that you express the pure emotion, hot off the griddle or hot out of the viscera, forgetting that the purest expression of emotion is a good healthy scream of ouch. But there is another paradox: we also have the notion harboring under the doctrine of "inspiration" that

descant

you don't express the self, but that you express a "truth"—you simply get in tune with a great truth—the redeeming blood, or the Party Line, or the New Deal, or on "native ground," or the Four Freedoms or the Great Society—and all else will be added unto you the moment you sit down to the typewriter. So we have the highly diverting spectacle of the "self"-gang, "the sweet-lyric-ouch" boys and the "oh-God-the-pain" girls, on the one hand, and the "truth"-gang, the "shut-your-eyes-and-damn-you-believe-it" outfit, on the other—whacking away at each other, when they are really members of the same family. Or we look back over the last thirty-four years and find that there were about 1930 a lot of quick-change artists, who belonged to the self-gang in the 1920s and the truth-gang in the 1930s, then switched again shortly after World War II.

We also have the corollary of the cult of infantilism and the cult of ignorance. This is inevitable, of course, for we are lazy and vain. But the reviewers flatter us in our laziness and vanity, and the great American reading public is always ready to take the next barefoot—and bare-brained—boy to its heart. That is inevitable, too, for our dearest myth is "from-log-cabin-to-white-house-myth." The only trouble is that we forget that Honest Abe sat up nights doing sums on the back of the shovel. But what should not be inevitable is the fact that writers who are not lazy and not ignorant feel compelled to adopt the pose. For instance, one of our best and most widely read writers fell into a fury some years ago when a critic remarked that he had apparently learned something from Defoe. The writer swore that he had never read a line of Defoe. Unfortunately, a friend betrayed the writer, and reported how he had done Defoe as bedside reading for a year. Then, further, there is the experience cult. Just go out and live and you will wake up some morning and find yourself famous. There was a time within the memory of the youngest present here when the little biographical note on the jacket of every slender volume of poems carried the information that Mr. So-and-so has worked as a police reporter, ditch-digger, and panhandler and his favorite recreation is beating up constables. Then there is another related cult—the cult of material. We have all heard some friend say: "You know, there never has been a novel about the moss pickers of Hoboken—as the case may be. I just know that would make a wonderful novel. I think I'll work it up."

But enough of this levity. The point is that in all of these cases we have a view which promises a gold brick to the writer, a short-cut, a release from artistic responsibility, which says, in effect, to the literary aspirant, "You can't learn to write—you don't have to try—the Muse, or the Four Freedoms, or America the Beautiful, or five love-affairs, or those fine old flea-trainers of Hoboken will take care of you—if you are one of the elect." And of course every one of us thinks that he is one of the elect. Every one of us feels something fine and beautiful bubbling up inside—we all have wonderful feelings. We just forget that everybody has wonderful feelings—everybody is just a great blob of fine, palpitating, delightful, tingling feelings. That's the trouble—everybody has the feeling, but everybody doesn't write "Lycidas." And it's not everybody who dreams "Kubla Khan." It was a man who was devoting a large part of his life to close thought on a variety of subjects—and among those subjects was poetry.

All in all, as far as English Literature is concerned, the exponents of this general view have been bad pickers. They pick Coleridge and Wordsworth and Milton to give them their texts. "Spontaneous overflow," said Wordsworth. "Simple, sensuous, and passionate," said Milton. And it sounds fine, until you begin to inspect what they meant. We can recall that Wordsworth also talked about thinking long and deeply and we can recall the heroic program of preparation which Milton set himself from early youth. He would turn over in his grave if he could hear how his phrase is usually applied. What he meant seems to me to be something like this: sensuous—in so far as art works concretely and not abstractly; passionate—in so far as art involves the feelings; simple—in so far as art is organized and can be grasped in its principle of unity and intelligibility, in its essential form. (But he would seem to mean that the immediate intuition of art—the grasp of the essential form—may come late and not early—after the effort of preparation—and not to all but to the fit though few.) In other words, Milton was talking about the appeal of art to the total being of man—sense, passion, intellect—about the healing of the

descant

breach in man's nature caused by the Fall. Paradoxically enough, the perverters of his phrase are those who would accentuate the split consequent upon the Fall rather than heal it; they would make art all "passion" on the one hand, or all "truth" upon the other. And, of course, they end with neither. And the story of Caedmon. If the voice said to him "Caedmon, sing!" the voice spoke to a man who was so thoroughly ashamed of his incapacity that he had gone out to the stables with its beasts. He had the proper humility, which is more than most exponents of the "let-down-the-back-hair" view have. And you can be pretty sure that Caedmon had been listening to the singing mighty carefully for a long time, too, before that night when he went to the stables.

So we come back to our original sophistical paradox after looking at the two views which are usually taken to evade the issue involved in it. Let us leave those evasions, and fall back upon our common sense. We know that we can't accept the first evasion, for we know that the rules won't help us. But we also know that principles may, and that principles can be grasped, can be studied. We know, on the other hand, that waiting for the Muse won't help us, or joining the Church or the Democratic Party. But we also know that there is a matter of native endowment, and, ultimately, a matter of miracle—but we can try to get ready for the miracle by the study of principle. Though we know that every good poem is a unique piece of exploration, that the solution can never be learned in so far as it is unique, and that after we have executed one masterpiece we have to start the laborious process of learning (which is the process of creation) all over again when we start the next one—unless we are to lapse into self-imitation, the most sterile form of imitation—though we know all of this, we do also know that there is a technique of exploration, that there is a study of principle. And this principle, this technique can only be mastered by the study of functional form—not form over here and content over there—but the relationship which is the poem, the novel, or the story. Happily there is a school for that. And here I shall quote a stanza from Yeats:

Robert Penn Warren

An aged man is but a paltry thing.
A tattered coat upon a stick, unless
Soul clap its hands and sing, and louder sing
For every tatter in its mortal dress;
Nor is there singing school but studying
Monuments of its own magnificence;
And therefore I have sailed the seas and come
To the holy city of Byzantium.

If we really study the monuments of magnificence, we shall no doubt become better writers. We might become better folks, too. And I suppose that is another way of saying that we don't want life for the sake of art (the fallacy of the "experience cult") but art for the sake of life.

descant

William A. Kittredge

The Cove
—from *descant* 12.2 (Winter 1968)

The cigar box was worn, the edges and corners rounded and the slick black finish softened by use, seemed fragile as an empty eggshell in his hands. Inside were a few black obsidian arrowheads, broken pieces of a collection he had as a boy, and a dozen or so file cards with football plays drawn on them in red and blue pencil. They were old high school single wing plays, patterns and number sequences he remembered even now.

One card, unlike the rest, was written on. The nearly formless scribbling he recognized as once his own ran uphill almost at a diagonal across the card. Three sentences, in numbered order, immature enough to make him smile. (1) don't laugh to much (2) finish Moby Dick and do your push ups (3) forget the kiss.

What kiss?

Alva closed the box and jiggled it a few times, listening to the contents jitter inside, then set it back on the windowsill.

The evening's final bronze sunlight was patterned on the river below the window. His mother's subdued voice, light and ironic, perhaps even resigned, heightened the quiet which had slipped into him, cut his wife's image like a sliver of honed glass.

The voice and image, emblematic of two parts of himself, which for years existed separate and equal and exclusive, tangled each around the other and around this, his childhood bedroom, and strangled his serenity in complex and interbound webs of love and impossibility.

The image of his wife . . . fresh cut grass sloping down from a provincial Japanese hotel, a drying odor of dew and clippings and fog dissolving out over the sea and, as they walked, forested islands seen through the changing perspectives of gaps in the interwoven clumps of twisted pine—and his wife, large with that first irretrievable pregnancy, skipping and then running somehow lightly down the carefully raked gravel path toward the endless rock shoreline and heavy breaking waves, scrambling onto an eroding boulder and standing frozen with the wind forced beach spray of salt heavy water blowing past and between her legs. Alva stood behind and out of the spray. Sunlight glittered on the flying water drops, and she seemed for a moment enveloped in rainbows of crossing color.

The formless orange shirt which had blossomed behind her abruptly clung to the curve of her swollen belly, the already kicking belly he bedded against. She looked back to him and her eyes, soft oriental when at rest, were brilliant and challenging, as they often were at the climax of love. The damp circumference of her turned neck and the glowing taut flesh over her cheek bones—all of her seemed luminous and elongated curving symmetry, perfect.

That was the first year, just after they were married.

Years later, one night in Alabama, when they were on the cement patio beside their concrete government house, each a little drunk, sipping gin punch over ice and listening to jet bombers go out in intervals toward some mock mission somewhere. It was quiet between planes and he could hear a moth batting against a window screen. His wife dropped the magazine she had been holding.

"I was happy," she said. "When I was pregnant the first time. I was a girl and I was happy."

His mother's voice pulled him back.

"So there's no chance of your staying."

Her tone implied no question, only fact. She was nearly sixty and sat obscured by the shadows of evening in the room, tranquil the stillness, holding her second scotch and water and curled gracefully against the blue and tan denim covered pillows on his narrow battered childhood bed.

"You're surprised?"

Alva Benson stood looking south from the wide second floor window, watching the last direct sunlight hang briefly and then rise from the trees in the sprawling lonely town on the far side of the river below. On the horizon, miles across the desert beyond, he could see the mounded tops of the Black Horse Buttes, still in the light and glowing softly near the peaks of Little Round and Craig's Top. For a moment this sight dropped him into childhood, and he was involved in a mystery of fragmented memories more real than the present. As a boy he had been going to climb those peaks with his father, but never had. Now that was another impossibility.

Tall and just past thirty, Alva was already softening. An officer in the air force, he had been a captain for seven years. Since college and Korea he had been in the service, briefly as a flyer and now as supervising officer in a photo lab.

"But I am surprised," his mother said. "Surprised and saddened." She lifted her hand and let it drop. Grace Benson, always thin and dark, kept the physical qualities he remembered, the light ankle and wrist, the slightly animal quickness and lack of common prettiness.

"Come home to be a man?" he echoed, smiling.

This room in the house above the river, where they lived since he was old enough for school, was the place he always imagined himself returning, the center place that was home on winter nights looking down and out at the lights.

Water birds were on the river, floating toward him from the west, emerging from beneath the black steel bridge. A flight of mallards, green headed drakes and dun hens, circled and set wings and joined the others there. Black and swanlike Canadian honkers cruised the slow center current. How many times as a child had he seen this, walked the tules along the edge hoping to find a cripple, come home muddy and cold to be warmed by her with chocolate before a fire?

"It shames me now. I'm deeply sorry and so is your father."

"That changes nothing. It's done."

"A family should have forgiveness. We are a family."

He turned from the window, leaned with his hands back against the sill. "There's nothing to forgive." He went across to sit beside her, rested his hand lightly on her knee.

She laid her hand on his. "You could come back."

"With my wife?"

She lifted her hand. "Is it that bad? That you must maintain such a defense?" She smiled. "I pity you in a marriage that must always be defended. Your father has been the pride of my life."

Years before, on a trip home, he sat with his father in the formal and ornate French living room off the lower hall and watched the smoke of his father's thin cigar settle toward the light blue ceiling. His father was a blunt heavy man, wore an expensive plaid wool shirt and manure-stained work boots.

"Responsibilities," the man said finally. "Yours are here. When are you coming back to take them?"

"Never," was the answer Alva intended, but did not then have the certainty to say. Now he said it each day, to either of his parents.

They had belittled the woman he married, despaired over the strange look of his children. He blamed his mother. She was the strength. Here, when he returned from Japan with his wife and the two little girls, began the wrecking of everything.

Now he was here again, settling last things.

He remembered small writhing fish, netted and struggling—seen on television—and the thin color of autumn light in the yards along the street following the river bluff, the everlasting look of the careful and ancient houses uphill across the street, the fading expanse of sloping lawns and scattered leaves.

"We'd better go down now," his mother said. "It's evening and you can have a drink."

He stopped a moment at the bottom of the stairs, fingering the carved newel post and the varnished banister curving up and away, thinking of all the times he had stood there and looked down the hall toward the door.

Even the invalid, his father, was quiet. They, the three of them that were the family, waited for the nurse to finish and go. She was quick with her smiling routine of temperature and pulse and blood pressure, swished as she moved, a young woman too clean and nearly pretty.

Alva turned away from the suspension of their argument, waited with his back to the others. Beyond the sealed window a flock of identical gray birds, small and quick, reminding him of his children,

descant

swerved and dove with mindless unity. Below on the lawn between the building and the sidewalk, an old man carried away piles of leaves in a canvas tarp. The street traffic was occasional and tranquil.

The slow door sighed and the nurse was gone.

"You'll change . . . your mother . . . the place . . . responsibilities . . ." The last word disintegrated into a sigh.

His father's head was back on the pillow, hanging with fluttering grained flesh. Everything here was full of drugs and dying. The huge and remembered cage of the chest, all that remained of another man, echoed words.

Urgent and wavering. "Go look."

His mother took Alva's hand. "Please," she said. "For him." Alva shook her away, but she grasped him again and finally he gave in, submitting like a hopeless aging virgin.

The heat was dry and still. The rim flowed and moved above them, undulating in waves of heat. Beyond that edge the sky was pale and reflected the yellow warmth of remembered grain somewhere ripe and falling. A dark speck that was a bird rose and fell, riding easily.

Alva and his mother stood in the deep canyon of Benson's Trout Creek, far back in the Black Horse Buttes, beneath the peaks he had once hoped to climb with his father. They looked down across a small dry meadow where the canyon widened.

The canyon walls were covered with dusty sage and clumps of bunch grass, marked by outcroppings of shelved lava and long slides of loose shale rock. Occasional junipers were scattered under the rim. The creek ran on the far side of the meadow and was bordered by turning willows and aspen. It was October and already the nights were freezing.

"You loved this place," his mother said. "I remember your pleading to come back. When you were a child."

"Not since." He squinted at the soaring bird. "I wonder if it's cooler up there?"

Miles south, where the mountains ended, was the desert. On the edge of that lower flat, astride the creek and using its water for irrigation, was the headquarters of his father's ranch. The little meadow before them had been cropped short by his father's cattle.

Alva and his mother had flown to the ranch that morning in a small airplane and landed at the dirt strip beyond the corrals. He took off and made the flight south, but she insisted on making the landing.

"So they can see I still exist," she said.

A loaded Jeep met them when they landed. Showing the fishing gear and the cooler filled with food, she was expansive and gay. Not like the old days," she said. "Now we go in style."

"But you go to the same old places." He carried the aluminum cylinder containing his father's bamboo fly rod. The old man had paid over a hundred dollars for it years before and kept it perfect, as he had come to do everything. Now he, Alva, the son, owned it and hated having it. The rod had been the one thing he openly coveted, allowed himself to speak of and then been unable to refuse. It was to him only a token of the man. Now it had been made a gesture, a major part of the old man's passing on, even the excuse for this trip.

"The old places are the best," his mother said. "Nothing can match these places, where you have lived."

"That's crap and you know it," he said.

She wiped her eyes and smiled.

Now they were here, in this place which was the oldest, the first he could remember. He wore new clothing bought for the trip, a creased flannel shirt and stiff Levis. His beard was dark and the hair on his hands stood out coarse against his pale skin. He felt completely away from his environment, faintly angered and unsure why he allowed himself to be maneuvered into something so far distant from his plans.

"It's yours," she said. "He's left you all the land."

"The heat in Algeria didn't bother me like this."

"Maybe you were thinner." She smiled and took his arm. Her shoulders had drawn forward into a slight hump these last years and her face was lined and perplexed until she smiled, but he could see no other changes, no weakening.

descant

Always he had flinched from these meetings of the will.

When he was small, not yet in school, she took him with her on a day's drive to the city. They were coming back. It was dark and late and he, the boy, slept in the back seat among the packages. A friend of his father's was coming back to the ranch with them, a man he could only remember as Uncle Red, a wandering and now forgotten man who sold firearms in those sporting days.

Alva woke to find they were stopped, parked in the deep moonshadow of the trees along the lane toward the ranchhouse. His mother was out beside the car with the man. Alva could see only their block figures against the black grass.

He crouched and pretended to sleep and did and then woke when Uncle Red was carrying him to the house. In the morning he came from sleep thinking of his mother gasping under the stranger. There was something awful gone wrong. Their own secret gathering was broken. Alone in the house with her, he asked. She smiled and ran a cool hand over his forehead, pushing back his hair.

"You mustn't say anything," she said. "Uncle Red would feel bad and leave. It's a disease."

His father and the other man and his mother spent the days quietly, the men hunting and his mother cooking and laughing at the things they said, sitting quietly on the porch in evening with a drink and looking from one shadowed face to another. Alva watched and saw nothing wrong. It was all right. She made it right and brought things together.

"Do you remember a man I called Uncle Red?"

"No, not at all. What would it mean if I did?"

"You should."

"All right," she said. "Red DeVore. Of course I remember. What does it matter?"

"It doesn't," he said. "I guess it doesn't at all."

The Jeep was parked at the end of a track road. At one time the road led completely around the meadow and ended at a small group of gray buildings and falling corrals near the lower point. Now it stopped at a dry wash the Jeep could not cross.

"We'll have to carry the gear down to the creek," she said. "It'll be cooler there." She began unloading, first pulling out their fishing gear—poles and nets and boots and creels—then the metal ice chest. It was filled with loose block ice and food in plastic bags, enough for tonight and the next day.

"I remember everything about that house," he said. "Even the snakes in the well."

"There was only one snake. The last summer."

"Was that why you left?"

"Not altogether. Snakes didn't bother us in those days."

Now there was a thing that could bother. His father dying in the white civilization of the hospital room. "Those great days. I guess nothing bothered you."

They walked down across the meadow, she carrying the fishing gear strung across her shoulders and Alva bringing the cooler. The grass, cropped short by summer cattle, was slick and dry on the rough tromped ground. A breeze came up the canyon and moved the dry aspen leaves.

"See," she said. "Always a breath of air here. It was always a fine place. I would never complain about living here."

"Like heaven."

"It was—the first place I lived with your father. I still think of this place as home, even after these years. They said I would never last, that your father was too hard. But I'm still around. Now he wants me to bury him here."

"For Christ sake. What use is this?"

She made her way down through the willows and waited at the edge of the water. He tromped heavily over the gravel washes behind her. The stream moved through a series of damming boulders, shining pools, ran thin over bars of gravel, bounced fresh and clean in the hot air. He settled the ice chest into a shallow eddy. The water was cold, but not the numbing chill he expected. He sloshed water over his face, then wiped on his shirt.

His mother sat on a rock in the shade of willows, the fishing gear piled at her feet. She pulled off her floppy hat and held it between her knees. "This was his private place," she said. "He always kept it chained and posted."

They had come through the locked gate miles back.

NO TRESPASSING FOR ANY REASON

"Like everything," Alva said. "Don't touch."

"That's his way. He kept things perfect for you."

"And now I don't want them."

"You want them. This is what you are. You learned to walk in that house. This is home."

"I have my own life. That's it." His wife and children, the two girls. They would be living in the enclosure of the concrete government house. She would have the doors locked and the windows shut tight, be existing with the air conditioning, having the first drink and frowning with a slight headache and fearing everything—the Negroes on the streets and the drinking water and the laughter from somewhere and the food in the stores. She would live enclosed in the shell until he returned and joined her.

"I came back because he was dying. No other reason."

She shuddered. "Here we are again."

He did not answer, instead lay out and began to assemble the fishing rod his father had given him. His father had forced him to kneel by the bed and put it together the day before in the hospital. Alva kept quiet in honor of death and did so like a child then waved it over the bed a few times to show he understood. In the midst of this, the old man lost interest and turned to the wall.

"It hurts him he can't take you out himself," his mother said, when they were leaving the hospital. "He can't give in easily."

"Who could?"

Alva stood in the other existence of the hospital corridor and took down the rod, for the first time experienced a choking sense of loss, grief more for an old idea of himself than for the man, dying father.

But now they were here, this old place above the creek, and he felt a little excitement at the idea of fishing again.

His mother stood and brushed the seat of her pants and began to work her way out of the channel. The breeze stopped, and it was very hot again.

Alva watched her walk and twist through the grasp of willows. She wore a man's checkered shirt and tight western pants. Turned away and moving, her hair dark, her body more youthful than her face, she might have been any younger woman, still supple and fluid. He realized he was seeing her as female and was surprised she looked fine from the rear. He ran to catch up.

The house was unpainted and weathered gray, the board siding warped and gapping and the glass gone from the windows. The door was jammed slightly open. The inside was torn and ransacked and littered with animal filth inches deep in places. Birds had nested among the rafters and their droppings were everywhere, on the iron stove and the fallen down table beside the window. Torn and swollen magazines were strewn in a corner.

Alva kicked through the pages, looking at old styles and different faces. His mother was in the doorway, her arms wrapped over her breasts. "What an awful thing. To see it like this." She shuddered and walked back into the sunlight.

"I kept it so clean," she said. "I scoured the stove every night and left it for this." She rocked herself against and looked away, down toward the creek. "He made me leave it. He said we would have better things."

"You've seen it this way before."

"Not really. Not before."

He left her there and wandered toward the barn and corrals. A slight odor of decay and dry rot was on the quiet air. A few surviving flies broke the silence. Since planning this trip he had been filled with memories of being a child here. He wondered now that they should be so distorted, that the relationships of inanimate things should have so transposed themselves in his mind.

The dry and warped watering trough was at the far end of the corral, contrary to his memory of it. He stood here and watched his father water the team, the huge man and giant horses.

"Your mother will be hunting you," his father said, but smiled and allowed him to stay.

Their long velvet noses sucked continuous thirsting gulps and sloshed in the water and then his father let him run his hand over

descant

their muzzles and brush away the drops and feel the nibbling lips, the searchings of their mouths. It was a team of massive geldings, a slow and spotted blue roan and a dark bay. There must have been others and he wondered what special gentleness fixed these two in his memory.

His mother was standing in tall rye grass below the half-collapsed barn, holding the stemless bowl of a briar pipe in her open palm. The grass was coarse and shoulder high around her. She stood over an old trash heap, a pile of animal bones and white deer skulls with gray antlers and broken castings off gone mowing machines, a litter of rotten boards and age-hardened harness leather gnawed by rats. The pipe was nearly white, the finish completely eroded. It rested softly in her palm, shell-like and somehow indecent.

"Do you think it was his?" she asked. "The horrible thing is, I can't remember." She bounced it lightly. "I don't remember if he ever smoked a pipe." She let the thing drop from her hand.

"It doesn't matter. You've plenty to remember him by."

Taking her hand, he led her from the trash, breaking a trail out through the giant rye grass. "Some things I have so secure, so plain," she said. "And others not at all."

Alva stood holding his mother's hand, looking across his father's little hidden meadow to where he could see the canyon of the creek out of sight. The mountains he had never climbed, the stream he had never fished with his father's pole, his mother's hand yielding in his, a childhood kiss he had forgotten, his wife's voice, his memory of her—her voice.

"I was happy."

The voice speaking, his own, startled him.

Coleman Barks

YELLING
—from *descant* 13.3 (Spring 1969)

like I just did makes me
think about it (Daddy, I
need to tell you something.)

COME OUT HERE AND TELL
ME (full resonance). Where
does it go? Surely he could
hear. But not, evidently,
with his head in front of
the big fan where he sleeps.

He repeats his need the same
sleepy way, testing how
the fan's breath takes hold

of his. BENJAMIN CAN YOU
HEAR ME. Do sound waves ever
completely stop? Think of that

sonic surf approaching
the stars. All the words
we've ever said out loud.

LISTEN YOU STARS YOU ALIEN
SONS YOUR DADDY IS CALLING
YOU AND HE WANTS AN ANSWER

J. M. Ferguson, Jr.

Spending the Day
—from *descant* 13.4 (Summer 1979)

Harry wasn't really Harry and his wife Ida wasn't really Ida. These were just names that came to Harry one fall day while they were driving along in the Sierras in their little blue Chevy with their blue-eyed daughter. Blue was Harry's favorite color. His own blue eyes, however, were often bloodshot now. He claimed they were a symptom of his anxiety, a condition that had plagued him strangely since the war. Ida told him he was a hypochondriac.

"Who would you rather be," he blurted as they climbed through Tioga Pass into Yosemite, "Edna or Ida Mae?"

"For Christ's sake, Merton," Ida scowled. "Do you have to start that stuff?"

Harry had an irrepressible way of coming up with questions that annoyed Ida.

"Which?" he insisted.

"Ida, I guess."

"Just call me Harry," Harry said. "I've always wanted to be Harry."

"Christ, Merton. You and Harry Truman."

When Harry had first come courting before the war and ventured his admiration for F.D.R., Ida's father had turned red around the neck and ordered him out of the house. Naming their daughter had caused a family crisis. Harry had wanted to name her Eleanor after Eleanor Roosevelt. "A great lady," he explained. But Ida had once known an Eleanor whom she detested, and besides her father had voted Republican for forty years. So they had named the baby Elaine, which Harry suggested as a compromise. It seemed to Harry that his life was composed of compromises with Ida.

"Harry and Ida," Harry murmured without satisfaction, his finger in his nose.

It was late September, and at that altitude the leaves on the aspen were already turning. The car had begun to descend into Yosemite Valley, and they had dropped into a rolling mist that was infiltrating the great pines. Harry really didn't know why he said such absurd things. He was a poet by nature and next to being Harry he would have preferred to be called Homer. A hawk was circling above them, and Harry could see that Ida was watching it, her face pressed sullenly against the car window.

"Harry and Ida," he said again, flatly. And the names stuck.

When Harry and Ida were married the war was already on in Europe. They lived in a small walkup apartment near the university where Harry was finishing his graduate work. They were poor and Ida was not used to it. She made the first months of their marriage miserable with her complaining and went home in the third month.

Harry decided to be grateful for the experience of cohabiting with a woman. It gave him a new perspective on things and made his poetry seem like the purest dribble. He decided to call it growth on his part. He watched the moon drop down his window and walked to his classes under the bare winter trees and thought he could always be happy in his celibacy. But then one night he had a dream about a girl he thought he had forgotten. Tall and blonde, she was his kind of girl. Harry had dated her briefly in his undergraduate days, and he had fancied he was in love, but then one night she had turned suddenly cold to him. Harry never knew why.

Ida was back after a week. Her father had turned red around the neck and told her to lie in the bed she had made.

Harry received her gracefully.

"Who would you rather be," he asked quietly, "Ralph Waldo Emerson or Henry David Thoreau?"

Ida looked at him queerly.

"Why?" she asked.

"I dunno," Harry said. "Thoreau never married."

"Henry David Thoreau, then," Ida said.

Harry nodded silently.

descant

As it turned out they both got their wish. Harry's graduate career was broken off before he could finish his dissertation on Henry David Thoreau. It was the year of Pearl Harbor and Harry was drafted by mid-term.

Ida cried when she saw him off on the troop train for his induction. Harry was touched. She went home to her parents to wait it out. Harry didn't see her again for five years.

Harry came home from the war looking tired and, of course, older. He had been unfaithful to Ida during his last years overseas. He had picked up a girl in the Soho district of London on the day Roosevelt died, but he did not tell Ida. His eyes were bloodshot, and Ida remarked on his disgusting new habit of picking his nose. Harry explained it all as a symptom of his anxiety.

Ida seemed to bear some grudge against him for being gone so long. He sometimes had the uneasy feeling, looking into her steel gray eyes, that she was uncanny. She seemed to have divined his infidelity, and Harry knew he would never atone for it.

Harry couldn't face any more graduate school. His father had died during the war, and he felt obliged to help his mother. Ida was jealous of Harry's mother and got herself pregnant in order to claim more of Harry's attention. So Harry took a job in a teachers' college out West. He spent his small savings on a used Studebaker. It broke down before they got there, and Harry had to buy the blue Chevy with money borrowed from the college credit union. Later he had to borrow more when the baby was born.

Ida found her first year at the teachers' college not much different from waiting for Harry in the war. There was never enough money, and when Harry was home he sat over a stack of papers to be graded, rolling his eyes distractedly and fingering his nose. Sometimes she wished she were dead, and she started to drink. She smoked a lot too, and when Harry came home he found loaded ash trays scattered all over the house. He couldn't get the smell out of his head at night and he slept fitfully. Sometimes in bed he had the feeling that Ida was glaring at him when he was half asleep on his pillow. They often quarreled before they could get out of bed in the morning.

84

"I'll be damned if I'm gonna sit around this house doing nothing all my life," Ida would say. "Why the hell do I need a college education? I wish I was dead."

Harry sometimes caught himself thinking it was too bad she wasn't, and too bad they let women go to college, except for the ones in his classes—Ida was suspicious of him on that count. Sometimes he would try to explain to her about education.

"That's not the point of education," he would begin. For a while he thought he would write a long philosophical paper on education, but he wore himself out thinking about it, and he was discouraged whenever he thought of all the people who were already writing about education. So finally Harry quit trying to explain.

They were both restless, and almost as soon as the baby was old enough they took to driving in the mountains on the weekends. But Ida didn't like Montana. She complained that it was too cold and that there wasn't any blue grass.

"Blue grass your ass," Harry retorted one morning before they had gotten out of bed. He rather liked Montana.

In the end, however, they went back East for Harry to work on his doctorate. Harry contended that he would never need it at the teachers' college, but Ida couldn't stand it any longer. It was one of Harry's compromises.

"Which would you rather be," Harry asked on the way back, "a two thousand pound Montana grizzly or a Kentucky thoroughbred eating blue grass?"

"For Christ's sake, Merton," Ida scowled.

Harry had his finger in his nose and his eyes were bloodshot.

Harry began to allude to his new "split personality" as he worked on his doctorate. He tried to explain that he didn't want to be a scholar but a poet, but no one seemed interested. Ida wasn't any happier in Kentucky, and although she complained herself she got tired of listening to Harry gripe.

"Go ahead and quit then," she would say. "I don't give a damn what you do if you'll get out and get some money."

"Get out and get me some money," Harry mocked. "It's the same here as Montana and it would be the same anywhere."

descant

"Go on back if you want," Ida taunted. "But you can damn well count me out."

Harry would have gone, too, but it broke his heart to think of parting from Elaine. She had Ida's dark hair but Harry's blue and sensitive eyes, and Harry couldn't bear to desert her. He felt sorry for her, knowing that his frequent quarrels with Ida struck wonder and confusion in her face. She seemed to be a nervous child and Harry feared she was developing asthma. Ida said he was imagining, but Harry felt guilty about it.

Harry noticed that his handwriting had begun to change. Sometimes, for example, he would print his s's, which he had never done before. But only sometimes, and without rhyme or reason, as far as he could see. Then he noticed that the same schizophrenia afflicted his capital D's and I's. Ida bought a paperback book on handwriting at the supermarket, but her only verdict was that Harry's r's indicated he was conceited.

It wasn't the handwriting itself, however, that disturbed Harry. He began to attribute his confusion to some frightening indecision and purposelessness in his character. The more he studied at the university the more often he found his meagre collection of convictions untenable, and Harry felt that he needed some convictions to sustain his identity. After all, he thought, wasn't it asinine to be confident about how to make one's s's when one did not know why he was bothering to make them at all? Distraction upon distraction seemed to prevent him from discovering the real answers. He felt that he was a man torn in two, but he didn't mention his handwriting to Ida again.

What he said instead was "I'm a man torn in two," and he read a passage from a book to her: "'Let us spend one day as deliberately as Nature, and not be thrown off the track by every nutshell and mosquito's wing that falls on the rails.' You know who that is?"

"Who?" Ida challenged.

"That's Henry David Thoreau," Harry beamed.

"Christ, Merton," Ida scowled. "You and Henry David Thoreau. I'm sick of that bastard." Harry had been quoting Thoreau to her while he was writing his dissertation on him.

"You really want to be Henry David Thoreau?" Ida taunted. "Then go be Henry David. I don't give a damn. You can get yourself a little shack and sit and roll your eyes and pick your nose and write poetry for all I care."

Ida was always saying something like that, but Harry knew some of it was true. He had read somewhere that his habit of fingering his nose was a symptom of his need for identity, and that there were certain sexual implications connected with it which disturbed him. Harry didn't tell Ida but he had taken to girl watching on the campus. He didn't know what Ida meant about rolling his eyes, though.

"Well," he said, "I don't know what you mean about rolling my eyes, but I'm sure as hell not writing any poetry. I never get a minute to write what I want, and all you do is gripe."

Ida was about to offer a rejoinder, but before she could Harry began to beat on his head with his fists in utter exasperation. Ida was concerned then and said she was sorry about always wishing she were dead—she didn't really mean it—and that everything would be better when he could finish up the degree.

"Yeah," Harry grunted. But in his heart of hearts he didn't believe everything would be better at all. Sometimes, sitting up alone at night, he was torn between working on his degree and writing a poem he had been nursing along in his head. He could do nothing but finger his nose. It was at such a moment one night that he caught himself rolling his eyes.

Harry never did finish his doctorate, and things didn't get better. He took a job in one of the California junior colleges he had heard about. He told Ida he could finish his dissertation "in absentia," which was a lie, and that they could move to a university somewhere when he finished it.

The pay was better than it had been at the teachers' college, and Ida was able to resign herself to her new situation except on Friday nights. She continued to smoke heavily, and Harry had to keep a bottle of bourbon in the house for her. It got to where Harry could count on coming home to a drunken wife on Friday nights, the nights Harry liked to relax after a hard week of teaching. One such night Ida didn't

descant

get supper on the table until nine o'clock, and when she did she got mad at Harry and turned the table over on him. She called Harry a son of a bitch and staggered off to her room and locked the door. Harry spent the night at his office, but he was finding it increasingly difficult to coax the poetry out of his soul. He didn't have much heart for his teaching, either, and he found himself watching the girls on campus more than ever. He was afraid it was becoming an obsession.

The life he was leading seemed intolerable. He toyed with the idea of becoming some kind of salesman so he could spend most of his time away from home. He thought of divorce again, but he still couldn't bear to abandon his daughter. She was then nearly four years old, and definitely asthmatic, Harry thought.

Harry tried to pacify Ida whenever he could on the weekends by driving her to scenic points around California in their little blue Chevy, and it was during one of the first of these trips, to Yosemite, that Harry thought of the names, Harry and Ida. Harry recognized that these outings were an escapist impulse, the same habit that they had fallen into in Montana. On one trip, in an out of the way green valley between some mountains, a man working with a hoe near the road raised his dusty face as they drove by and showed them a healthy animal smile. Harry couldn't get the man out of his mind. He made him think of some of D. H. Lawrence's characters. He knew their little excursions were only temporary stays—from what, he was not sure—and he was usually anxious about a stack of themes left behind that had to be graded. He felt his life slipping through his fingers while he drugged his spirit with the beautiful scenery.

"Who would you rather be," Harry blurted one Sunday afternoon while the sun was going down, "Henry David Thoreau or Lady Chatterley's lover?"

"Jesus, Harry," Ida snapped, "watch the road."

Harry quit his job abruptly in the middle of his second year at the junior college. He never offered any explanations. He came home one afternoon mumbling something incoherent in a hollow sounding voice and flopped into a chair with his finger up his nose. Ida questioned him, but Harry only said "I have nothing to teach." That was all she could get out of him.

Ida wrote to her mother that she suspected Harry was having an affair. They had been to a party not long before he quit his job and Ida had seen him slap a willowy blonde on the buttocks. Harry drank himself into oblivion on gimlets and went around telling everyone he was throwing his hat into the ring for the presidency. He cited some Chief Justice that Ida had never heard of as a distant cousin. It was election year and Harry Truman had announced his plans to retire. Harry found employment as a technical writer for a corporation in Sacramento that was doing secret defense work for the government. He had to pass a security clearance to get the job. He found the work boring and the routine tedious, but he was beyond caring and he never complained. Ida thought it was the best job he had ever had: it paid the most money. Harry realized there were easier ways to make money than teaching or writing poetry. He began to work overtime on Saturdays.

But again Harry's job ended suddenly. He was working overtime one Saturday when his supervisor caught him fornicating in a broom closet with one of the secretaries. Ida heard about it from the supervisor's wife. Harry made feeble allusions to his anxiety, but he didn't try to deny it. Both Harry and the secretary were dismissed, of course, as poor security risks.

Ida took Elaine and spent her six weeks in Reno, and then they were back to the blue grass country to live with her parents. Harry found himself alone, divorced, and saddled with a judgment for alimony and child support. He was still carrying the debts he had incurred at the teachers' college, transferring them from one credit union to another as he moved about.

It seemed to Harry that the world was being run by Republicans, who had won the November election. And he felt guilty about Elaine.

Harry did his best to pull himself together. He had long nourished a secret desire to be single again, but time was suddenly heavy in his heart. He didn't feel young again, as he had imagined he somehow would. He was just thirty-four, and he knew that he was not too old for a new beginning, in spite of five years wasted in the war. Yet he felt his back against the wall, and his anxiety was unalleviated. He

descant

had more time for his poetry, but he couldn't find a poetic phrase in his head. He began to send out some of his old poems to editors, feeling that it was time he tried to publish something, but they came back one by one, rejected. He finished off Ida's cigarettes and the bottle of bourbon she had left—he had had to ship a whole crate of her things to her. When these were gone Harry bought another carton, and another bottle.

He needed, he knew, a good job in order to meet his obligations and maintain himself. He wanted to be able to send a check to his mother once in a while, but he had little hope of helping her. He knew he was all washed up as far as security clearances went, and his only other thought was for the business world. Harry didn't relish the idea, but there wasn't any line of work that really appealed to him. He wrote to as many college textbook publishers as he could think of, and he finally landed a job with a big company as their Midwest representative. It didn't pay as much as he had hoped, but he thought he would manage if he stayed in the second best hotels and saved some of his expense money. He rented a small furnished room for himself in Kansas City, the site of his company's regional office. It was an old building inhabited by elderly people, but he didn't mind because the rates were cheap.

Harry had one more brief affair and a chance for a second on his new job. He was in line by himself in a Kansas City cafeteria when he heard someone behind him calling his name. It was one of his former students from Montana. They had lunch together, and she explained that she was working as a beautician—she had never finished at the teachers' college. Harry remembered that he had never been able to picture her as a teacher, and he also remembered that she had sat in the first row of his class with her skirt pulled casually above her knees. She had nice thighs, he remembered, and she was not unattractive in a rather plain and insensitive way. Harry thought that for the relationship he had in mind it was fortunate that she was not especially sensitive. When he told her he was divorced she volunteered her phone number.

The first time he called her they spent the night in Harry's room—she had two girl friends sharing her apartment—and the following day

Harry was served an eviction notice by his landlord. Harry changed his mind about old people for neighbors, and he began to wonder whether he had some kind of proclivity for making his lovemaking public. He took another place nearby, but in the end it turned out to be more than he could afford, and he had to move again. He missed the peace and quiet of his first room, and only then did he realize how well the place for old folks had suited him.

Harry never saw his former student again. He had to travel shortly after their first date, but he called her again one winter night after he had been to a cheap theatre that showed burlesque films. One of her roommates told him that she had married. Harry was a little stunned. He wished that Ida would marry too, and take the burden of alimony off his back, but then Harry couldn't recommend her to anyone.

Harry had a chance for a second affair with a young woman who was an instructor at the university in Columbia, Missouri. It was early March on a Friday afternoon, Harry's favorite time of the week, and he was in her office trying to interest her in a textbook. He looked up and noticed that she seemed more interested in him. She had taken off her glasses and was smiling at him. Harry was suddenly aware that she was an attractive woman, but she looked sensitive and intelligent and maybe a little too slender for him. He decided she was not his kind not at the moment, anyway.

"Well," Harry said, "I have to make St. Louis tonight. I thank you for your time."

It was a lie, of course, and she put on her glasses and quit smiling.

Later, walking up the Strollway and looking in the shop windows on his way back to his hotel, Harry wished that he had at least asked her to dinner. On the second floor of his hotel he could see men and women embracing behind drawn shades. It looked for a moment like a Roman orgy, but then everyone suddenly changed partners and he remembered the dance studio, which operated there at odd hours. Starlings were clustered on the building ledges, making a tremendous racket as the sun went down. The still luminous sky southwest of the earth silhouetted black branches of elms that loomed on the horizon of the city like a network of roots by which the planet clung to the universe.

descant

Then it was dark and Harry felt lonely.

The following September Harry was forced to go to a finance company to meet his obligations to Ida. He tried to adjust to hotel rooms that were worse than second rate, but he found them too depressing. In one, in a St. Louis hotel where an exposed light bulb hung down from the ceiling on a cord, he smelled flesh in the bathroom. Later, taking a bath, he discovered on the edge of the tub several large callouses that someone must have pared from his feet.

He was passing through Columbia on a Friday night, and on Saturday morning he strolled about the campus, hoping faintly to see again the woman who had smiled at him. The campus was quiet, and as he walked Harry felt an emotion he couldn't name. Turning a corner, he thought the woman who came into view on the walk ahead of him might be her.

He presumed she was on her way home, but before she left the campus she entered a building that looked only recently completed. Harry followed cautiously, with curiosity and longing, thinking he ought to be framing an alibi in case he should come suddenly upon her, yet unable to do so. Within the building there was the smell of fresh paint and plaster, but no living being, as far as he could determine. Then he heard a noise echoing from a far stairwell. Pursuing it, he looked with surprise down the winding metal stairs which must have descended several stories below the ground. He hesitated before plunging into what his imagination kept suggesting was some secret tunnel he had discovered to the bowels of the earth. For an instant, Harry was struck by the incongruity, the implausibility of his situation, as if at that moment he were removed from and observing himself. He felt unalterably alone then, his longing overcoming his uneasiness, and he descended the stairs in search of the noise he had heard, of which some person, he reasoned, must surely have been the source.

At first he saw no one. The stairway ran into a closed door, and, opening it, Harry thought he had reached a cul de sac. He stood before a dimly lighted room of metallic shadows that he recognized as boiler room equipment, and he was about to retrace his steps when he heard the noise again. Something moved in the dim room and emerged between amorphous pieces of dark machinery. He was confronted by a white-haired, trembling figure: a wrinkled, molelike old man in gray janitorial attire, leaning on a mop. Harry felt the squinting eyes fasten upon him inquisitively.

Back in his hotel room, alone with his bourbon, Harry wondered what the woman at the university had seen in him in the first place. He had noticed that his hair had begun to thin. His eyes were bloodshot, and he thought his nostrils seemed slightly enlarged from his nervous habit of picking them.

"I could never afford to marry her," he said aloud to himself in a voice that was strangely hoarse. He hated himself for having preferred the beautician, his former student, to this young woman.

He dreamed that night again of the blonde of his college days whom he had loved. She was as tall as Harry. They met at a party, in a room full of people, and later, leaving together, she pressed close to Harry and told him she had never been able to forget him.

Harry awoke unnerved by the fact that she should occur in his dreams again. Remembering how abruptly his romance with her had ended, he thought now that he could understand why.

"Can it be," he asked himself, "that she knew me better than I knew myself?"

Later that fall things went from bad to worse for Harry. He didn't keep to his traveling schedule for his company. He went anxiously to his burlesque films and he spent long hours in newsstands looking at girlie magazines. And he bought more bourbon.

He was staying in a motel in Joplin when he came down with the flu—he hadn't been taking care of himself. For two days he just lay in bed with his bottle and a fever. He got back to his office three days behind schedule and found himself dismissed. His supervisor told him the company wasn't satisfied with him anyway.

It occurred to Harry that all he had in the world were his clothes and his books. With a kind of perverse and defiant logic he gave all his clothes, except an old army trenchcoat and the ones he was wearing, to the Salvation Army. He donated all his books, except Henry David Thoreau's *Walden,* to the nearest library. He notified his landlord that he would be out the following day. Then he went to the burlesque theatre and saw a marvelous big stripper whose flaming red hair hung down to the small of her back.

"You marvelous big thing," Harry sighed to himself after he had begun to drink in his room. His mind wallowed freely in his lust, and he was tormented by a desire to relieve himself. He tried to think of something else he wanted to do.

Harry started to read Henry David Thoreau's *Walden*. He read the last chapter first, and he lingered on the part where Thoreau described the butterfly coming out of the farmer's applewood table, like some kind of resurrection. Harry wondered whether Henry David Thoreau meant to imply a resurrection, and whether he could be resurrected, himself. He didn't believe in immortality. He surmised that Thoreau must have been talking about a man's potential in this life, and thinking about his own life, Harry saw how he had succumbed to shameful sensuality. It was no good, he knew, blaming it all on his anxiety. He decided then upon a pilgrimage. He would hitchhike to Walden Pond and spend the rest of the winter there, where Thoreau had lived a century before.

But then Harry read the introduction to Walden by a scholar in his own century, and when he finished he was sorry he had read it. The scholar explained that Thoreau's pond had been made into a public beach and that authorities had found that the pond ranked high in urine content among the waters of the greater Boston area. Moreover, he advanced the Freudian theory that Thoreau's practice of immersing himself in Walden Pond was a manifestation of his suppressed sensuality.

Harry decided not to go to Walden Pond after all. He remembered how blue the water had looked when he had last passed by the Lake of the Ozarks, and he decided to go there instead. Blue was Harry's favorite color.

Ida told the investigator that she didn't know whether Harry could swim or not. She had never seen him try, but she thought that he probably could and that he was just pulling a fast one. The investigator explained that a copy of *Walden* with Harry's name in it had been found in the boat drifting near the middle of the lake. It was a big lake and they might never find the body, he said. It had happened before.

Ida's alimony stopped coming and there was nothing she could do about it. Harry's body was never found in the lake, but it couldn't be located anywhere else either. She felt a little uncomfortable about Harry and about the drifting boat. She decided she would forgive him for deserting her. Besides, her father had died and she had inherited all she needed for herself and Elaine.

Ida taught Elaine that her father had been a disgusting creature and that she should never, never trust any man. Harry had often feared she would teach her something like that.

descant

Denise Levertov

Red Snow
—from *descant* 13.4 (Summer 1969)

Crippled by desire, he questioned it.
Evening upon the heights, juice of the pomegranate:
who could connect it with sunlight?

He took snow into his red from cold hands,
it would not acknowledge the blood inside,
stayed white, melted only.

And all summer, beyond how many plunging valleys,
                              remote, verdant, lesser peaks,

still there were fields
by day silver, hidden often in thunderheads,
but faithful before night, crimson.
He knew it was red snow.

He grows tall, and sets out.
The story, inexorably, is of arrival
long after, by dark.
Tells he stood waiting bewildered
in stinging silver, towards dawn,
and looked over abysses, back:
                      the height of his home, snowy, red,
                      taunted him.

Denise Levertov

Fable snuffs out.
What did he do?

He grew old.
With bloodbright hands he wrought
icy monuments.
Beard and long hair flying,
                    he rode the whirlwind,
                                  keening the praises
                                          of red snow.

descant

Richard Snyder

Sestina: Letters from a Girl in the Peace Corps
—from *descant* 14.1 (Fall 1969)

Some shy unrest cut deep into my mind
like unhealing initials carved with dates
in classroom arm chairs, cabalistic signs
far more tangible than winnowing words
of lecturers. Unquiet dogged my days
like nagging duty vaguely realized.

My soft times accused me. I realized
that what had gone unhealed within my mind
to cut across my grained and varnished days,
and carve my calendar to nagging dates,
was my shallow, scheduled life bound by words,
while I, gone sulky, sly, sought other signs.

All my codes had come from books, all were signs
for someone else but hardly realized
by me who could no longer feed on words,
on fish-food paper. I would put my mind
to something more than study, skiing dates,
all the ciphers of my winnowing days.

My parents those bright spring-vacation days
when I told them, shut off the set, gave signs
of bewildered hurt, then calendared dates
until I left them. They had realized
that their serpent daughter had set her mind,
had gone word-deaf, even to their sad words.

Richard Snyder

Then only the letters, more paper words,
footnotes to my elemental days
of work and wounding heat. I did not mind
in my dark interior peace such signs
as black accosting eyes I realized
I once feared from bandstands on dancing dates.

Dust and rain and tedium turned my dates
to Conrad's *job sense,* dull joy beneath words.
The natives' passivity realized
some restive yearning from my former days;
their oxen patience, their squatting grace, signs
of stubborn beauty carved into my mind.

Now beyond those dates, back to former days,
reading Conrad's mere words and old desk signs,
a new unrest realized in my mind.

1970–1989

❧ Introduction

"A girl cries out: 'Yes! I want to change my life!'"
from "Poetics 105," Joyce Carol Oates

In the '70s and '80s, two of the most tumultuous decades of the twentieth century, millions of people embraced the dreams of change, and these currents of possibility touched millions of Americans. Like the student in Joyce Carol Oates's evocative story, they felt the desire to change even if they lacked the capacity to effect a real change. The eighteen writers in this second *descant* section were some of the most powerful voices in the twentieth century to examine how Americans, culturally and individually, negotiated between the possible and the practical with the impossible and the impractical.

By a rough count, the eighteen authors in this second section have collectively published nearly three hundred books, truly an impressive and culturally significant number. Joyce Carol Oates, one of the most prominent and prolific authors of the last three decades, has herself published over one hundred books, an astonishing and significant oeuvre that has imaginatively engaged thousands of readers—and which continues to engage. Among the eighteen writers are some of the most read and discussed literary authors of contemporary print culture. Authors such as Oates, Betts, Inez, Madden, McDonald, Rogers, Ruffin, Sanford, and Thomas have all been important and highly regarded influences, and in publishing their work, *descant* makes its unique claim to being one of the leading small literary journals of the late twentieth century.

Historically, the period of the '70s and '80s began with the disillusionment that followed the burst of idealism that had swept the country in the early '60s with the election of John Kennedy as president. The United States not only had to deal with Kennedy's assassination, and then as well the equally shattering assassinations of Martin Luther King and Bobby Kennedy, but also with the deep dissensions and divisions that occurred over the Vietnam War, the civil rights movement, the feminist movement, and indeed all of the movements of protest. The idealism of the '60s had turned radical, contentious, and violent in the '70s and '80s. The sad, tragic end of the Vietnam War, especially the haunting images of the chaos and loss during its final days, was quickly followed with the disillusionment of the Watergate scandal and Nixon's resignation. People across the country waited hours for gasoline during the Arab embargo and watched with mute rage as American hostages in Iran were paraded before television cameras. The myth of American invincibility was shattered under the combined weight of the endless social, cultural, and political turbulence of the '70s and '80s.

The writers of *descant* reflected on their culture with a steady, unflinching gaze. Their poems and stories evoke powerful feelings and reveal a great depth of emotion. There is an astonishing range of human experience in their texts, although there is considerable probing of death, mortality, and loss in their various assessments of the human condition. From the natural to the unnatural, from the pastoral to the municipal, the writers of *descant* offered evocative insights into the intricately woven tapestries of life observed and imagined. Yet what is striking about these texts is not their capacity to decipher and resolve, but their capacity to engage and charm. Each one of these poems and stories demonstrates the aesthetic power and beauty of words, and each one attests to the writer's ability to transport readers through the literary experience. The different journeys readers experience might not always be pleasant, such as to a hospital ward for mutilated Vietnam veterans, but they are always powerful, and thus they are always pleasing.

–Daniel E. Williams

Colette Inez

Remembered a Mustang She Rode to the South
—from *descant* 14.2 (Winter 1970)

Furlongs in the southland,
red from weeping winter long,

lantana in flower,
she and the mustang
loping away
from the mildewed voices

into rivers and moats
her mind could swim.

When the mustang pulled
toward home,
she saw the town
accountable,

a shriveling ray,
the sun
foretelling darkness—
and the stolen pony
returned to his reins.

descant

Greg Kuzma

The Porcupines
—from *descant* 14.2 (Winter 1970)

The moon is opening little patches
in the woods, picking out the silver
shapes of two porcupines
going out to eat, down from their
trees where quick daylight
threatens them. At night they
creep in the pace that keeps them
fat; rolled over on their backs
an easy prey to claw and tooth.

Afoot like dinosaurs, they move

a nerveless path, or will they
mind the cold since fur and scale
have come together at a point.
Theirs is the beginning of
a kind of quiet defense
we are looking for. At night
their eyes go big with the calm
that has filled the world. In
daylight the road stops them,
humped in conclusion, marking
the edges of our progress.

David Madden

A Human Interest Death
—from *descant* 14.3 (Spring 1970)

Edward Savage's father was gassed in World War One. He spent twenty years dying in the veterans hospital at Kingsport, Tennessee. Until young manhood, Edward lived with his mother and his older sister, Helen, on a farm in Cades Cove in the Great Smoky Mountains. His mother was never too severe nor too conciliatory about his needs, his moods, his ambitions. Helen worked in nearby Maryville, a country town fifteen miles from Knoxville, in a dime store, and set aside a portion of her meager salary for Edward's education, to supplement earnings from his rural morning paper route. Declared too short for service in World War Two, he attended business school in Maryville.

In Knoxville he met a waitress at the Gold Sun Cafe on Market Square. Anticipating his marriage to Reba, an enormous woman from Hazard, Kentucky, Edward went to work for the Public Utilities company in Knoxville as an accountant, his first and last job.

When Edward's mother died, and Helen moved to Knoxville to be near him, Reba personally auctioned everything off: the mountain farm, the furniture, anything that would bring a nickel. The only thing she allowed him to keep was his mother's wicker rocking chair. But she wouldn't allow that "countrified old rocker on the front porch for all the neighbors to laugh at." Edward wanted to screen half of the front porch with a lattice and let honeysuckle climb it, a reminder of the farm and of his mother and sister, but Reba said, "I'll be damned if you will."

For twenty-five years she would harp on the same theme: "Why can't you move up in the company, up the ladder of success, instead of always quivering on the bottom rung?" Edward merely waited, and things happened to him. He was given a few little raises without asking. He had a son without even trying. He was never able to explain

descant

his apathy to Reba, but her constant nagging and his son's sullen contempt were more lucid than any answers he could have invented.

Still, he always told himself, his was good, clean, steady, honest work. Besides, look at the next-door neighbor, Jim Logan. An aggressive man, a hunter, a fisherman, a bowler, a poker player, an American Legionnaire. How far had he gone? After all these years, Logan was still a bus driver for the Knoxville Transit lines.

But not even having an imbecile daughter had made the Logans unhappy. When Dennis was in high school and Myrna was growing up (she attained her full height of five-six and a weight of one-ninety by age eleven), Edward would come into the house on a cold winter night to find Reba and Myrna seated before the TV. In the summer the obese girl would be sitting on the grass at Reba's feet, while she reclined in her deck chair with a Royal Crown Cola, reading *Forbidden Romances* aloud by the failing light that slanted across the lawn. Every morning on cold days, Edward lugged in coal to last until noon. Then Myrna carried in buckets of coal so Denny wouldn't have to do it when he came home from school.

There were times when Edward wished he could go hunting with his son (although even when he was growing up in the mountains, he had not enjoyed hunting). But his son was content to take Reba to ball games, to laugh at her vulgar jokes, to listen to her retell the troubles of the people in the *True Romances*, to fetch her underthings and stockings from the clothes-line.

Edward's house was on the last street along the side of Sharp's Ridge. One night just after he had made love to Reba and was sinking into sleep, a thunderous crash woke him. Naked, he followed Reba through the house to the living room window. They watched a plane high on the ridge burn until daybreak. He asked Reba to pray with him for the pilot, but she laughed at him and pulled a hair from his belly.

A few days later, a telegram came, informing them that their son, Alfred Dennis Savage, had been killed in Vietnam "in defense of his country."

The next morning on the bus, Edward watched rain dash against the window. Even for a rainy autumn morning, it was very dark. A kitten, soaked to the bone, was walking very slowly in front of the Methodist Church which Edward attended regularly, keeping a promise to his mother.

All day, making entries on the books at the utilities company, Edward thought of the cat. When he came back on the bus that evening, the sky was still gray and his feet were wet and cold. The kitten was walking in the same direction in front of the church, still wet.

With hasty pity, Edward got off the bus on the corner at Rose's Drug store. When he stooped down, the kitten walked into his opened arms. Trudging up the hill, he held it inside his overcoat, feeling its icy wetness, its fitful breathing against his heart.

From the bed, where she lay reading *Secret Confessions,* Reba yelled, "Off with them galoshes! You're tracking up the floor." She had not mopped it in weeks. When Edward opened his overcoat, dramatically revealing the little animal, Reba screamed, "Throw that mangy thing out of here!"

"I–I brought him for *you,* honey. To–to keep you company now Denny won't be–"

She laughed contemptuously. He realized lucidly for the first time how much he hated this woman. But he did not throw the kitten out. Within a month, the alley cat was like a third person in the house, and Reba's baby-talk nauseated Edward.

Myrna often went to the store for Reba. And if she did something wrong, like bringing salt instead of sugar, vinegar instead of Royal Crown, or needles instead of hairpins, Reba was not abusive. But after Denny was killed, she was capable of making her eat the salt, drink the vinegar, and of jabbing her buttocks with a needle. At night in bed, she often bragged to Edward about her hold over the girl, excusing herself on the grounds that Myrna worshiped her and was insensitive to pain and mockery.

On top of Sharp's Ridge a silver tower flashing a red beacon had been erected to warn planes not to fly too low. Edward found an odd comfort in watching it. It seemed a personal sign of everlastingness, a reminder that his heart beat red and wet in the dark cave of his chest, but, also, of his dreary, day by day existence.

Many Sunday afternoons over twenty-five years, Edward went out to the coal house and, in the clothes he had worn every day to work and to church, he sat rocking back and forth, remembering how it had been on the farm in the Smoky Mountains. With the acrid smell in his nostrils, the dry hiss of coal dust under the rocker, he hated Reba for hiding his clean "Sunday best" to prevent him from getting away from her nagging to go see Helen. To dispel the hatred, he imagined the smell of honeysuckle that had loaded the lattice on the porch in the Cove.

One Sunday in early spring, Edward rented a car for an outing in the Smoky Mountains. Reba made him steer clear of Cade's Cove, but she enjoyed the sprawling tourist town of Gatlinburg. Her face seemed the essence of youth and innocence, her stomach was great with child. And he stole fond glimpses of his wife as he drove up into the mountains, covered with wild flowers and budding trees.

After the picnic, he picked some wild roses for her in a thicket by a stream bulging with boulders, and took a snapshot of her sitting, like a girl, on a rock, her feet dangling in the foaming, racing water, the huge luscious roses nodding in her arms.

That night, when they returned home, he paused at the door, pretending to search for the keys, accumulating courage to kiss her. He did kiss her—full on the mouth, then awkwardly unlocked the door. No sooner were they inside than she, confused and surprised by the bold kiss, began to reproach him for not leaving the windows open to let in the spring air, and, with the cat following at her heels, she made a bee-line for the bathroom.

Sitting morosely in the kitchen, he tried to shut his ears to her shrill voice, announcing that he had failed to get toilet paper the day before at Kroger. The cat was in her arms when she came out, sharpening his claws on the red sweater over her stomach. She strode into the bedroom, slamming the door behind her.

Edward went into the bathroom. Clinging to the inside of the porcelain bowl of the toilet was a wet rose petal.

Two weeks later, after long, agonizing, sleepless nights, Edward walked out of the Public Utilities company building and turned reluctantly toward the Gay Street Bridge. A small crowd was hovering over the railing. Behind them, a motorcycle lay on its side against the curb. Edward, painfully embarrassed to find a crowd, edged to the rail. Below, on the still, brown water, he saw a small object. A fat woman at his elbow said it was a motorcycle cap. Edward got so nauseated by what the people around him said about the man who was somewhere deep under the Tennessee River that he almost vomited on the fat woman's arm.

That night, he thought briefly, and rather nonviolently, of ways to rid himself of Reba. But amid hopeful thoughts of the child, near the threshold of life, he abandoned such furtive thoughts.

For a while, he feared that the child would be a boy, a sort of resurrection of Dennis. When they brought the baby to her, Reba looked at Edward with a new contempt, mingled with bitter resentment, as if to say: So now you are so old and dried up and useless, all you can give me is a girl, instead of a boy to compensate for Denny's death. Edward smiled, faintly. That set her off. She went over each of the baby's features, calmly, in seeming good humor, as any mother might, and for a moment he felt: Perhaps I was wrong about the look on her face and in her eyes. But he heard her saying how peculiar the mouth, the eyes, and the chin were, since they resembled neither his nor hers.

Having no answer to that, least of all a smile, he turned and looked out the window, down at the snow on the ground.

Soon after she returned from General Hospital, Reba struck Myrna across the face with a flyswatter and screamed at the top of her lungs, "I don't ever want to set eyes on you again, you fat idiot!" Edward felt for Myrna the pity one feels for an abused animal that seems human. No more did Myrna enter the house with that silent suddenness that had so disconcerted him.

Reba insisted on naming the baby herself. Edward was shocked and then delighted when, in her deliberate ignorance of anything to do with his past, she named the child Lucy, which was also Edward's mother's name. As Lucy grew and her resemblance to Edward was unmistakable, Reba stopped tormenting him with doubts about her paternity, but turned instead to undervaluing the child, remarking that she was getting cross-eyed, that she wasn't bright, that she might

descant

even become another Myrna. During these moments he did not speak but fastened his eyes upon Lucy and felt pride and tenderness and joy for the first time in many years. At last, something had come of his marriage that, by virtue of Reba's own crudeness and spite, was his alone. But Reba found many ways to destroy his bliss.

He would look at Myrna's father, Jim Logan, who sat behind the wheel of the bus, and think: Poor man! Yet, he's better off than *I* am. Even though I have Lucy, I can't love her in peace.

He didn't see Myrna very often in the neighborhood for several years. But sometimes as the bus crossed the Gay Street bridge over the railroad yards, he caught a fleeting glimpse of her walking down the tracks between the boxcars in the bright evening glow. He would hope: perhaps she is going away, far away and never come back.

Sometimes at night, Edward heard Jim call to his little boy, Gene, and they would get in the car and go in search of Myrna. Edward imagined them finding her wandering back toward the ridge along Central Avenue, walking as in a trance around telephone poles, and collecting cigar butts from the gutter to give to her father as presents. And Gene, sitting in front, would exchange a look of understanding with his father now and then as they drove homeward with Myrna in the back seat.

But sometimes at night when Edward went to pull the shade to prevent the red beacon from keeping him awake, he saw Myrna sitting in the bushes in the shadows cast by the moonlight, watching the window, even when snow was on the ground. And several times in the morning, when he raised the shade, she was standing just outside the window, and though she looked at him, she seemed to see nothing.

One morning, having abruptly pulled the shade to blot out this terrible sight, he turned to walk out of the room. He happened to catch a glimpse of Reba's sleeping face, and it occurred to him that she resembled Myrna. He stood at the door several minutes, looking at her. Her mouth was open in that perpetual, stupid expression Myrna wore. Having kissed his sleeping child, and put coffee on to boil, he went back to look again because he wanted very much to disbelieve it. He found the cat, lying on Reba's heaving breasts, his green eyes staring, full of indifferent contempt.

When Lucy was three, Helen and "good ol' Bill," her husband, a successful insurance salesman, moved to New York. To Edward, it was as if they had moved to the North Pole. Once in a while, she sent him a letter and reminded him not to forget to put flowers on their mother's grave on Decoration Day. And he felt guilty and ashamed because he had never forgotten, but he had never done it, either, even though he now had a car.

One Sunday, Edward and Reba and Lucy took a drive into the Great Smoky Mountains. It was a very dark but pleasant, cool, starless night in March, the wind singing at the open window. They were just beginning the descent from Clingman's Dome, the highest point in the Smokies. As usual when returning home after having been half civil most of the day, Reba was ridiculing Edward for his failure to become more important in the public utilities company and for showing Lucy too much attention while ignoring *her*. Thinking of his child sleeping in the back seat, Edward suddenly trembled with love for her.

And as usual, Reba told him to stop at one of the pull-offs so she could relieve herself in the darkness behind a tree. Height always affected her that way.

Obediently, embarrassed, even in the darkness with no sign of a car, he pulled over, shut the motor off, went around and opened the door for her, and then got back in and started to scoot over under the wheel again when he heard a sharp, sudden scream, followed by a longer scream that tapered off like air going out of a balloon. After almost five minutes, frozen with terror and disbelief, he got out of the car and carefully walked to the edge of the shoulder of the road.

There he found a flat rock. A feeling in the pit of his stomach told him that after that there was nothing for a thousand feet. He did not know how to respond. When a car stopped with a flat tire, he was laughing.

Lucy did not wake up even when the ambulance came and the crowd of tourists became noisy. But with the first glow of morning light on her face, she opened her eyes there in the mountains, and looking up into Edward's weary eyes, said, "I dreamed of fields of yel-

descant

low daisies."

When she heard of Reba's death—it was a "human interest" death, so she read it in the *New York Daily News*—Helen cabled a bouquet of roses, though Reba had once threatened to beat her to a pulp for alienating Edward's affections. Edward flushed them down the toilet.

As the preacher intoned endless words of praise for "this pious, good woman, this faithful and serving wife," Edward felt remote in mind and body.

The day Reba was buried, he cut up her deck chair for fire wood. He calmly ripped the striped canvas cloth from the frame and tossed it into the cat's box. Then he sat before the fireplace rocking in the wicker chair. The next morning, he found the cloth coiled around his shoes at the foot of the bed. Somehow that incident prevented him from carrying out his intention to call the city pound to take the cat away. The next day, he built a lattice and planted honeysuckle.

A few months later, using part of Reba's insurance money, Edward bought Lucy a new dress and a new tricycle.

Even before he opened the screen door, he smelled the honeysuckle. Overwhelmed, he stood at the end of the long, dark hallway, inhaling, his burning eyes shut. He would not smoke his usual King Edward this evening. He wanted to enjoy the flower's nostalgic odor and the pale yellow blossoms, hanging abundantly from the lattice that walled the porch off from Wautauga Street, while Lucy rode her new tricycle in the front yard. He sat in his mother's wicker rocker and let the coolness of the late summer evening soothe his eyes. His glasses lay on his stomach, the ear pieces held lightly in his fingers.

Rummaging gently among the vines he found a blossom, plucked it, and sniffed it so rapturously that it clung freely to his nostril a few moments. Then he sipped the nectar from the stem. Absently, he put it in his vest pocket next to his watch below his heart.

Through the vines, which blurred the moonlight and the streetlight, he saw Lucy in the fresh cut grass, riding her tricycle in the blended, pulsing lights. Now and then, he heard her soft voice speaking to herself, or to the greenish blinking glow of lightning bugs, gliding on the air, maybe to the tricycle itself. The words blended, too, sounding like a strange, comforting music, along with the crickets and the faint squeaking of the wheels, soothing in the background. He couldn't see her clearly, only her golden hair and her soft, new yellow dress faintly, moving beyond the openings in the tender vines. He knew it was late and she should be in bed, but he couldn't think of breaking the spell.

He wished the red light, blinking over the tower on the crest of Sharp's Ridge like the heart of an animal, worrying the nervous tremor of the stars, would stop pulsing. But as long as it was dark it would not stop. The light intimidated and mocked him. Yet he knew that if it were not there, another plane would crash. His belief that Lucy was conceived the awful night of the crash would not leave him in peace. He was still reminded of it by the black space on the ridge which five summers had failed to make green. Perhaps the honeysuckle would grow thick enough to shut out the prying eye of the red light, as if Reba were still watching contemptuously his every mood, mocking his contentment. He inevitably lapsed into counting one-two-three infinity, one-two-three *infinity*, and when he really got started he couldn't stop until it became unbearable. "One-two-three infinity," he began, a slow whisper, tapping his glasses on his stomach. It made him think now of his work in the office, of the endless years of copying into a black book for more ambitious men to give meaning to.

Through the jungle-like growth between his house and Jim Logan's Edward looked into his neighbor's living room. Even now, looking at this scene disturbed him. Sitting in his own easy chair, Jim smoked one of his many pipes, reading the *Knoxville News-Sentinel* that his young son Gene delivered. His wife Grace sitting on the sofa across from him, stopped knitting and Jim looked up from the paper to admire her work. She smiled, and, though the back of Jim's head was toward the window, Edward knew he, too, was smiling, saying something nice to her. That's life, Edward had been telling himself all his life. Some men get all the luck.

He was glad Myrna didn't walk across the room, shattering his contentment with her obesity, her uncannily graceful walk, her long,

descant

tangled black hair, her nothing-seeing eyes. He could not be glad enough that Myrna's insatiable curiosity, or whatever passes for it in the warped mind of a sixteen-year-old imbecile, had not embraced Lucy.

A sound like a car back-firing startled him. "Must be those damn little hellions and their drag races! Got to be careful about Lucy playing near the street, wandering out of the yard like she does. Ought to call her in before too long." He thought of Lucy, of her endearing past, of her enchanting present, her glorious future, for the fulfillment of which he would work, aspire, and achieve, save, provide, plan, fight off any and all obstacles.

Aware of the creaking of his mother's rocking chair, he speeded up the tempo, smiling at the fact that no one could nag him out of it. He took the wilted honeysuckle blossom from his vest watch-pocket and sniffed it again. That the fragile blossom had already begun to decay disturbed him. Then his eye caught the red blinker again. "One-two-three *infinity* . . . ." He counted until he could no longer endure the monotony, that element in his experience which, above all else, he wanted to destroy.

Suddenly, he stood up, knocking his glasses to the floor. Groping in the darkness, he found them, not broken. But something green and luminous pulsed on the glass over his left eye. He was still so unnerved by the blinker that instead of immediately brushing the thing away, he counted: "One-two-three *infinity*." As Edward stumbled into the long, dark hallway, his throat very dry, the firefly flew out into the yard.

He stood leaning back, his buttocks pressed against the sink, a glass poised in his hand, tepid tap water in his mouth. It occurred to him that a good deal of time had passed since he had last heard the musical sounds of Lucy at play in the yard. The cat walked across the hall, coming from Edward's bedroom, going into Lucy's. Something about its arrogant, arthritic stride and the sudden way it turned and looked at Edward, startled him.

Suddenly afraid, he ran out the back door, the glass still in his hand, and descending the steep back-stairs, called Lucy anxiously. He quickly looked in and behind the coal shed, then ran, stumbling in the gullies in the yard, to the front of the house. At the sight of her, sitting lumped over the bars of her tricycle in a posture of sleep, he felt relief coupled with a milder feeling of foreboding.

But as he approached her, he knew something was wrong. Standing over her limp body, he stared at a large dark spot in her blond hair, a thick tendril that spread down her nape and on down her new yellow dress, settling around her small buttocks—a dark red pool on the green metal.

The next day, Edward sat in the living room with a detective, the windows shut, to keep out the suffocating odor of honeysuckle. When someone knocked at the door, the detective answered it for Edward. Jim Logan, his hand on Gene's shoulder, walked in.

"Mr. Savage, my son has something to tell you." Logan stepped backward and leaned against the wall just inside the door and listened with Edward and the detective to what his son was saying.

Gene told of a breach of his father's trust, for which he was very much ashamed, and of the consequences. "Last night I went up on Sharp's Ridge to shoot at tin cans with my daddy's rifle. Halfway up, I heard somebody following me. By the light of the moon and the tower light, I could see Myrna climbing up the path. I told her to go back but she kept climbing, and it's so steep and loose you wouldn't think she could. She came on up to the top where I was standing, and followed me across the path to the other side, and I told her if she would promise to go back and leave me alone I'd let her shoot first. I gave her the rifle and pointed at a beer can on a log, but she raised the barrel toward the sky with this queer look on her face, like she was scared to death, and she was aiming right at that red beacon light, and she pulled the trigger and missed."

Gene walked over to Edward and stood before him. Looking him full in the face, he told him that he was sorry and that he wished his sister weren't the way she was, so she could tell him herself that she hadn't meant to kill his little girl.

But Edward was only half listening. He was looking at Jim Logan on whose face shone an expression of pride for his son's strength of

descant

character, and shame, with forgiveness, for his son's disobedience.

"Mr. Savage," said Logan, "if there's anything in all the world I can do . . ."

That evening, Edward tore down the honeysuckle and the lattice and pulled the rocking chair into the living room. The next day, he buried his daughter. A week later, he took the rocker back to the coal house. The following week, the cat died of old age. Edward is retired now, in excellent health, and he still lives in the house. He doesn't pull the shade against the pulsing beacon light.

Doris Betts

Peripheral Vision
—from *descant* 15.2 (Winter 1971)

Late in Jerusalem summer
William Blake, back from the dead,
Came ablaze in my head like uranium.
We lurched through my unified room like some
Uprooted lighthouse. Numb—
But radiant. Every man's thumb in bloom.

Albion's children were streaming to Woodstock
Interlocked, Blake nor I neither could sleep
While they dreamed by, translucent,
Every bone gleaming aloud.
Thus did the cherubim shine!
(Or the Gadarene swine.)

"Heaven and Hell are unwed?" Blake engraved
Such grave lines in my head that it ached.
I preferred the opaque by far
To the sight of Earth's heavenly burning
With Blake and me, turning in light,
Like two summer stars on a star.

descant

Walter McDonald

Cam Rahn Bay Hospital Surgical Ward 2
—from *descant* 15.4 (Summer 1971)

>Piece goods all in
>white
>line the walls
>remnants all
>the rest of us
>gone—
>eyes pieces of guts and
>gonads
>legs and arms
>all gone
>are the gonads of yesterday
>the wind has
>blown them all
>away. We are such
>stuff as jackals feed
>on and our
>long time growing
>is gone
>when will they ever learn
>gone
>are the days
>my heart
>was young and
>gave blood to
>My *legs where are my*

Walter McDonald

There there
the nurse soothes
There there
where are my legs of
yesterday
(whispering)
wind from
a rocket's red glare
(o say can you see)
has queerly blown them all
gone.

David Bottoms

The Door
—from *descant* 17.3 (Spring 1973)

When I saw the blue ambulance
back up to the apartment door
and the driver emerge
with no apparent regard for haste,
I knew it could only mean death.

Policemen began to arrive
and neighbors gathered gradually
to form a gallery in the yard,
until the door
was the final barricade
between the curious and death.

Though it was a door
into a darker world,
most remained still.
Only now and then
would a photographer pass from the light
to flash a hint of revelation
back through the curtains
of the living room window;

David Bottoms

or would a well-dressed man
who might have been a minister,
more probably a detective,
shuffle in and out of the darkness
and never reveal the mystery.

Though it was a door
into a darker world,
most remained still,
talked, smoked, and depended
on reporters, policemen, and detectives
until the ambulance
carried the body away.

descant

Kelly Cherry

Ashes to Syllables
—from *descant* 17.4 (Summer 1973)

1
For my love
who is burned
to death. He
did it him
self, cracking
his sweet skin
over live
pink coals. He
did not know
how to be
cool, nor to
be ginger
or beware
pretty sparks.
This light fall
of words, to
make a small
epitaph
and to wrap
his smoking
bones from my
eyes. Where what
screaming they
do will be
smothered in
to silence.

Kelly Cherry

2
It was not
that he was
not to be
seen where we
whispered in
the owl's dark
nor that his
eyes closed as
clouds closing
in on us
bringing black
rain down fast
nor in fact
that his arms
ended where
his hands ought
to have been
the leap of
antelopes:
it was that
when we re
versed our
direction,
there was no
sign of him
anywhere.

descant

Paul Ruffin

Female Cousins at Thanksgiving
—from *descant* 20.3 (Spring 1976)

    The old Thanksgiving game
        has brought them to the country
        to Grandma's house,
        the full table
        and ageless talk of ageless aunts
        and uncles and things
        that used to be.

    Boys ring the woods
        with man sound, their
        long shadows knifing the fields
        for rabbits and birds, their
        guns rolling the hills
        with rhythms of the hunt,
        the dance of young gods.

    From the smokey, too-hot house
        the girls slip
        to loiter in the sun
        at the edge of the back porch;
        a radio tinkles between them,
        the fields lie before them,
        and then the woods and hills,
        the smokey distant shapes of boys.

Paul Ruffin

Talk goes round in the thick room,
    the television shows a ballgame,
    bellies and memories are full;
But lean boys slip
    through the woods, intent
    on grey ghosts
While the girls huddle outside,
    whisper and giggle
    and wait for a glimpse of the gods.

descant

Annette Sanford

Nobody Listens When I Talk
—from *descant* 20.4 (Summer 1976)

Locate me in a swing. Metal, porch type, upholstered in orange-striped canvas by my mother. I am spending the summer. My sixteenth, but the first I have spent in a swing. I could say I'm here because I have a broken leg (it's true I do have pain) or ear trouble or a very strict father. I could say I like to be alone, that I'm cultivating my mind, that I'm meditating on the state of the universe. I could say a lot of things, but nobody listens when I talk, so I don't. Talk. Not often anyway. And it worries people.

My mother, for instance. She hovers. She lights in a wicker chair by the banister and stares at me periodically. She wears a blue-checked housedress or a green one under the apron I gave her for Christmas with purple rickrack on the hem. She clutches a dustcloth or a broom handle or the Woman's Section of the *Windsor Chronicle*.

"Marilyn," she says, "a girl your age should be up and doing things."

Doing things to her is sweeping out the garage or mending all my underwear. Doing things to me is swimming, hanging on the back of a motorcycle, water-skiing. To her, a girl my age is an apprentice woman in training for three meals a day served on time and shiny kitchen linoleum, but she would be happy to see me dancing the Funky Chicken if it would get me on my feet.

I stay prone. I don't want to do her kind of thing, and I can't do mine. The fact is, I don't fit anywhere right now. Except in a swing. So here I am, reading.

My father arrives in the evening. He has worked all day in an office where the air conditioner is broken, or with a client who decides at five minutes to five to invest with another company. He flops in the wicker chair and communes with my mother's ghost.

"Marilyn," he says, "a pretty girl like you ought to realize how lucky she is."

Lucky to him is being sixteen with nothing to worry about. My father grew up in Utopia where everyone between two and twenty dwelt in perpetual joy. If he were sixteen now he would have a motorcycle and a beautiful girl riding behind him. But it wouldn't be me. If he were sixteen and not my father, he wouldn't look at me twice.

From time to time my friend comes. I give her half the swing and she sits like a guru and pops her gum. She can do that and still look great. When she blinks, boys fall dead.

"Marilyn," she says, "'a girl like you needs a lot of experience with different men."

She will get me a date with her cousin. With her sister-in-law's brother. With the preacher's nephew from Syracuse. She will fix me up in the back seat of a car with someone like myself, and we will eat popcorn and watch the drive-in movie and wish it were time to go home. I could say, *"I'm not that kind of girl at all,* I could say, *someone should be kissing me madly, buying me violets, throwing himself in front of Amtrak for want of my careless glance."*

Who would listen?

So I say, "No." I say, "Maybe next week." Then I lie in the swing and watch the stars come out and wonder why I didn't go.

When you lie in a swing all day you remember a lot. You close your eyes and listen to the locusts humming in the elm trees and you think of who you are.

You think of you at six, crying into a blue corduroy bedspread because your uncle has laughed at your elephant which has no tusks. You have drawn it as a gift for him. You have never heard of tusks before.

You think of lying in the big iron bed at Grandpa's house, listening to the cistern water tapping on the stones outside the window, knowing you are safe because you are the baby and everybody loves you.

You think of the Dancing Class Grand Ball when you are twelve in a pink dress with ribbons in your hair and a head taller than the boy who brought you. His mother has made a corsage for you and when you dance it rubs against his nose. You pretend he pulls away

descant

because of this, but when you are sixteen lying in a swing, you know it was the scent of your own self-doubt mingling with the rose and lavender that sent you to the chairs waiting by the wall.

When you lie in a swing all day, you live in the world you read about. You drag a bare foot back and forth across the floor and hear the song the chains sing, but you aren't really you.

You are a woman standing by a table, reading a letter from a box of other letters. A dead man wrote them. His face, as young as yours, he has given to the baby sleeping by the window where the boats pass. He has dreamed his own death and written a passage from the Psalms . . . *his days are as grass, in the morning they flourish, in the evening they wither and are cut down.*

You are a father counting cracks in the sidewalk passing under your feet. You have waited a long time in a railroad station for a train carrying the child who walks beside you, who says: *my mother made me come even though I hate you.*

You are a girl, pregnant, alone in a car you have parked on a country lane. You are kin to the brown cow chewing across the fence. *You are wet and sticky and blind, curled in the cow's stomach waiting for your birth.* You are sick in the ditch.

You are a boy in a room with bars on the window, an old woman on white sheets looking at the Good Shepherd trapped in a frame, a child with a scar on his face.

When you aren't really you, then the who that you are is different somehow: strong, and part of everything . . . sure of a harvest for every season . . . glad to be sad. You are a riddle with hundreds of answers, a song with a thousand tunes.

When you lie in a swing all summer, fall comes before you notice. Suddenly elm leaves pave the street, and you have been seventeen for three days.

It is time to get up.

In the kitchen my mother is still in her apron, frying the supper steaks. I sit at the table and eat a grape. I could say, *don't worry about the underwear. When the time comes, I can mend it. I can cook and clean a house and love a lonely daughter. I was watching all the time.*

Instead, I yawn, and she looks at me. "A whole summer," she says, and shakes her head.

In the den the weatherman is promising rain. I kiss the top of my father's head where the hair doesn't grow anymore and lay my cheek on his whiskers. I could say, *I really am, like you said, beautiful.*

"Try something light for a change," he says, and hands me the funnies. I curl on the couch and call my girl friend. She tells me she has kissed a trumpet player. He has an incredible lip. She tells me bikinis are on sale, blond men get bald first, mud is good for the skin.

I could tell her, *summer's over.* I could say, *men are born and die and are born again. The rest is only details.* I could say,

roses are red,

violets are blue.

I grew up,

but nothing happened to you.

I don't though. It hurts too much. And besides, nobody listens when I talk.

Sometimes not even me.

descant

Pattiann Rogers

How You Came
—from *descant* 21.3 (Spring 1977)

It's a wonder how you came
Clear across a city,
Jumping the roofs of marble towers
Like stepping stones,
Weaving under metal girders,
Tripping up orange steel,
Bolts as big as sausages.

Like a billy goat over bridges,
Ignoring dark trolls and their gleaming spikes,
You were brave
In the black beneath concrete viaducts,
Their undersides pinned with the brushwork of birds
And dripping the green of last week's water.

Past a thousand, thousand wooden doors,
You circled the rooms of glass buildings,
Skirted cement walls,
Walking sideways just above rivers.

You balanced like dusk,
Even moss couldn't cause a stumble.

Without pebbles or string,
Without magnets or stars,
Without even my line
Blue on white paper,
You came,
Found your way at last
Turning, like a branch bent quick in the wind,
The latch at my very window.

Joyce Carol Oates

Poetics 105
–from *descant* 22.1 (Fall 1977)

First-floor landing of the old Whitbread Memorial Building, one winter morning: a pudgy girl in a green wool cap is talking animatedly with another girl. Wound about her neck is a bright green muffler with long fringes. There is a tassel on the cap—she shakes her head and the tassel flops about cheerfully. Flushed with cold or with excitement, the girl has reddened cheeks and very bright eyes; her voice is shrill and solid at the same time; she stands blocking your way, not seeing you. Her camel's hair coat is soiled and rather wrinkled, as if she has been sleeping in it.

She turns—glances at you as you attempt to squeeze by—and then her look takes hold, seizes you, becomes an intense delighted stare.

"Oh," she cries, like a child, "oh—it's *you!*"

The leaded windows of the classroom look out upon a windswept snowy scene: the small quadrangle appears unfamiliar, drifted with odd shapes, and across the way the library is barely visible. Girls enter, stamping snow off their boots. You get things ready for your class in poetics—always, it is necessary to pull the heavy lectern back to the center of the room (the professor who teaches at 9:00 always shoves it into a corner), and to erase the blackboard of his scrawled hieroglyphics, which are, this morning as every morning, laughably incomprehensible. The girls are settling down now, talking in low urgent voices, several are pulling ski-jackets off, over their heads, and one, standing, is brushing snow from her slacks. Then a shrill voice surprises everyone—and you turn from the blackboard to see her, the girl in the green wool cap; she hurries into the room, her unbuttoned coat now flapping about her.

"God! Am I late? Am I—? The clock in Fletcher Hall must be five minutes slow! I hope to Christ—Is it always so dark around here? This time of day? I mean—I am in the right class, aren't I?"

descant

Her questions fly without direction; she flops down in a front-row desk, turning it partway around in her excitement. She unwinds the green muffler, looping her arm about her head, carefully—round and round—the muffler must be six feet long!—and then folds it, carefully, and puts it beneath her seat. "This is Poetics 105, right? Meets Monday-Wednesday-Friday at 10, right? *God!* Am I lucky the Dean let me register late! I have the damndest wildest freakiest luck sometimes! You know," and here her voice becomes a whisper, she is evidently addressing several of her classmates, "you *know*—this is a rare privilege for us, it's a fantastic honor and opportunity—to study with—"

You are leafing through a book, nervously, aware of the girl now jerking her chin toward you, in a touchingly child-like gesture. She has been speaking to Molly Brady and Jane Holbien, two of the outstanding students in the class. "—with *him*. A genius. I mean—it's fantastic, isn't it? Literally fantastic? I can hardly believe it! I was sort of sick, you know, missed the first term and was very depressed, I lost fifteen pounds which was the only halfway tolerable thing about it—couldn't keep a goddam thing down, that's how sick I was for a while!—the doctor didn't want me to leave home, my parents either, but people like that are always very conservative, you know, they always are! Had to fight like a minx to get my way—but—but here I am!—no small accomplishment, in my opinion! Actually enrolled in a poetry course with *him*! Do you guys appreciate the fact that a genius is actually teaching this class? A *genius?* The Dean didn't want to let me in but I hacked away for forty-five minutes and—"

You clear your throat to speak. "Perhaps—we could begin class now." But how disappointing!—your voice is strained, perplexed, nearly inaudible. "Perhaps we could—"

The girl claps her hand over her mouth. Her alarm exaggerated, she swings the desk back into place; her shoulders are raised, her lips now pursed, in an attitude of caution and awe. But as you speak on certain formal matters—a paper due the following week, the arrangement you have made to put several rather rare books of yours on reserve, in the library, for their use—she begins to rummage through her big leather purse, muttering to herself. *Now where did I—where the hell is—*A notebook with a bright red cover appears. Then she rummages for a pen. *Where the hell is*—But no luck: no pen. She has to borrow one from Molly Brady.

And now—

But someone calls *Yoo-hoo!* out in the corridor—and the girls in your class giggle—and before you can go to shut the door, the pudgy girl fairly leaps out of her seat to shut it for you. "Allow me, sir! Allow me!" she murmurs. She tiptoes back to her seat and picks up her notebook and pen.

Twenty-five girls in Poetics 105, and all are now staring at the pudgy girl in the green cap. She, by contrast, seems unaware of their curiosity—she sits on the edge of her seat, pen poised, ready to take down anything you say. She is staring at you through her red-brown eyelashes, alert and expectant.

It is after 10:00; it is time to begin.

This morning you intend to discuss—

You ask a question about the relationship of form to content in a sonnet of Donne's.

You clear your throat and rephrase the question and—

Silence.

Their eyes are downcast. Even the new girl, leaning over to read the poem in Jane Holbien's text, is silent.

You rephrase the question and—

There is Doris Shay—rimless glasses and a small, intense, pretty face—Doris who usually responds to your leading questions: now fussing with the zipper of her parka, avoiding your gaze. There is Maureen Prentice—and Maryanne O'Rourke—exchanging tiny startled smiles. At the back of the room, near the radiator, Jocelyn Clark slouches in an enormous fur coat—a ratty hulk inherited, she has told you, from her grandfather who wore it to football games long ago, long ago in New Haven. She frowns, pretending to reread the poem. No response.

You cannot resist looking at the girl in the green cap. She is reading the poem, her lips moving, her head dipping in irregular enthusiastic nods; evidently the poem delights her. The wool cap is perched rakishly on her head, its tassel swinging now over her right ear, now out of sight, now over her forehead. The green is too bright for her complexion, which is sallow, sickish. Only her cheeks are flushed.

descant

Except for her eye make-up, which is elaborate, she looks like a plump twelve-year-old boy—her red-brown hair peeps out from under the cap, styleless, unevenly cut, her mouth is small, her nose tiny, "cute." Something puppyish about her. Something piggish. Small pink-scrubbed pig. *Content to form, relationship of,* she mutters under her breath. Her sweater is bright red, like the cover of the notebook; her skirt is one of those expensive tartan skirts, pleated and adorned with an immense mock safety pin. Her legs appear to be muscular, rather than fat; her boots are unfashionable—mere ankle boots, badly stained with salt and mud.

Her hand leaps into the air. You cannot look away in time.

"The essential thing is, in determining the relationship of content to form—I mean, the fundamental assumption would have to be unless I'm very much mistaken and have misinterpreted your question, sir?—a basic philosophical issue—metaphysical, actually—one must ask from what perspective, from what *a priori* theorum, the question has been made?"

Fairly bouncing in her seat now. Eyes glistening.

The other girls look from you to her, from her to you, in amazed silence. You try to summon your thoughts—try to remember many years ago, a young man still in your twenties, hadn't you dealt with such an issue?—in an essay published originally in an English journal, then in *Poetry?*—and hadn't you concluded that brilliant, witty essay by saying—

But the girl interrupts; apparently her question was only rhetorical.

"For instance, sir, if we improvise a bit and make the question a local one, in regard to your own poetry, I mean—if that's agreeable!—I mean in regard to your superb first collection, which I agree with—what's his name—who was it—that critic in the *Times* the other week—by far your finest work—the other three books not *quite* as impressive, not as energized by that distinct primeval vision—though of course technically beautiful!—beautiful indeed—in a context of so much contemporary ugliness—The question is intended to initiate a primarily subjectivist exploration of the possibilities of a genuine dialogue of Self and Other is perhaps misleading, isn't it? Or am I off-base? It won't have been the first time, so just let me know!—But if it relates to the essential and even *organic* drama of time and the eternal—that is, content and form—I think—don't you?—the question lands us squarely on radical ground. And that's good. We must acknowledge the artist's unshakable unspeakable *faith* in his work, you know, what James must have meant by the donnée, and what he certainly meant by setting forth an almost Lévi-Strauss structuralist metaphysics in his more important Prefaces—the art-work as a verbal creation—a thing—a unity in which individuals cease to exist except as they compose scenes—though of course one might hypothesize that the scenes do not exist either—that in fact *nothing* exists, apart from everything. And so—"

At this point the girl grins. She looks around at the other girls, as if they might help her phrase her remarks; as if she were speaking for all of them.

You start to speak. You say, "Excuse me, but I really think—"

"Hey, let me *finish!*" she laughs. "You know, the famous thing about this college—the real selling point, in my opinion—is that free and open and intimate discussion is encouraged—isn't it? I mean, even if somebody registers two weeks late—due to illness—due to uncontrollable circumstances involving a weight-loss of many pounds—hospitalization for thirty-nine God-awful days—inability to keep anything down on my stomach and bleak black days of depression—well!—all I was saying was—your original question, though vaguely worded, might—I only say *might*—be a legitimate one considered in the light of a Jamesian position—by which I mean that there isn't actually *anything but form*. Any old content would do, you see. *Any old anything!*—That's all I meant," she says. Her voice is now quite meek.

You will not survive.

Suddenly it is clear—utterly clear. The completed thought presents itself to you, in your own interior voice. *You will not survive this class.* . . . In the margin of your book there are innumerable lines and doodles. Who has drawn them? You, who have always considered books sacred?—books of poetry (whether your own poetry, or others') especially sacred? Who is perspiring, who is so suddenly anxious? Who is trying to fashion a reasonably sane smile—?

descant

Molly Brady is hiding a smile of her own. Jocelyn Clark, long-legged, and lazily beautiful, is smirking; she is watching you closely. The girl, unaware of the other girls' attention, takes advantage of the silence again. She frowns, tapping at her front teeth with the pen. "Perhaps if my remarks were re-worded—made more simple—But of course the essence of the problem is unwordable—it refuses to be, you know, put into words—that is, *worded*. Like poetry itself. Oh sure—the 'future of the written word' and all that bull—the 'faith of the artist'—I'm alluding quite liberally to your speech, I guess—that big speech you gave when you won some award—didn't you?—I mean, wasn't that you?—or someone else?—well—well, I'm quite aware of *that* post-Humanist ploy, but what about the future of the *future*? Have you given much consideration to that? Have you maybe been discussing it before I got here?—This is really a fantastic place! There's a dozen or more geniuses teaching here—the rumor has it that some of them are finished, of course—*kaput*—long past their prime—but still so iconoclastic and fascinating, like all geniuses—but *you*, sir, are the real reason I fought my parents and the doctor—this course in poetics might be a turning-point in my life, I told them—I fought like hell to get into your senior honors seminar, but no luck—I realize I'm not quite qualified, but—but, well!—I always hack away, always give it a try, you know?—I mean, what have you got to lose, right?"

Your small sane smile does not waver. You gaze at the girl, nod very gently—as if none of this alarms you, as if you are even humoring her—and look away, out into the faces of the girls. Such attentive faces!—such fine, hard-working girls! A few of them are brilliant, you've been surprised and pleased with the course so far, and perhaps—it might be a relatively simple strategy just to call upon one of them, as if nothing unusual were happening this morning—as if you had not encountered a pudgy shrill creature in a bright green cap out on the landing, as if she had not followed you into the sanctuary of this classroom—"Rhoda?" you cry. "Miss Blair? What is—what do you— Have you any comment—?" And suddenly you are staring at Rhoda, pleading and cringing—and begging her with your eyes to speak: but she does not speak. Rhoda, to whom you gave a rare A+ the semester before: now startled, frowning, brushing her straight black hair out of her eyes, refusing to look up. She mumbles something. You cannot hear. You ask her to repeat it—she mumbles again, resentfully—and again you cannot hear—and still she won't meet your gaze, won't acknowledge your kindly, desperate soul. Rhoda? Molly? Jocelyn? Jane? If someone would—

Silence.

Words swim; you are staring at your book; unrelated lines of poetry spring into focus, and fade; words soar, scramble, careen, pop, sink, flash, shudder, burst, shrink, evaporate, turn muddy, shoot into focus again—and again fade, before you can interpret them. Words?—a string of words?—a small art-work of words, constructed solely of—of *words*? Is it possible? Was it ever possible?

At the prime of your life, in Room 354 of the Whitbread Memorial Building, on a cold snowy Monday morning in January, you notice that you are smiling oddly at a stranger's voice: smiling, as if hoping for sympathy, at her glittering eyes. You are unable to recall why you are here—what you are doing—what you were engaged to do—how this has all come about—who has just spoken or will speak—her, or you? You, or *her*?

"Hey," she says excitedly, "just flipping ahead a few pages, just by accident I—can I borrow this book?—thanks!—I have the crazy idea I just answered my own question. Do you mind? I mean, if I read this? It's from an old favorite of mine—just a few lines from it and I think, I think we might be in the clear. Okay? Okay if I read it?"

You nod helplessly in the girl's direction. But she has already begun, in a firm, rather histrionic voice:

> "So charming ointments make an old witch fly,
> And bear a crippled carcass through the sky,
> 'Tis this exalted power, whose business lies
> In nonsense and impossibilities:
> This made a whimsical philosopher,
> Before the spacious world his tub prefer,
> And we have modern cloistered coxcombs, who
> Retire to think, 'cause they have nought to do.
> But thoughts were given for action's government;

Where action ceases, thought's impertinent.
Our sphere of action is life's happiness,
And he who thinks beyond, thinks like an ass."

"I mean—wow! *Wow!* That's really it, right?"

For the duration of the poem her voice was transformed; now it grows shrill again, her face gleams piggish and cute. Her eyes!—iridescent violet eyeshadow—heavy black lines outlining the lids—lashes spiky, red-brown as if dyed—the gaze warm, wet, glittering—sisterly and yet coquettish—arch, intellectual, daring and yet maternal—bullying—quivering with—No, she is nothing like this: she is a stranger; she is inexplicable, unwordable.

She seems to be awaiting—? A response—?

Your voice is fairly normal. It must be made louder, that is all. But normal, normal. Just listen: "Yes—certainly—certainly a way of—of approaching—The paradoxical nature of—Dialogue of—Necessity for—And," and here your voice seems to catch hold, to become an adult's voice once again, "and—detachment—intellectual, critical, holding-at-arm's length of—the classical, the Augustan, demeaned in our time but—certainly—an authentic response to—Yes, and perhaps some of you noticed, did you?—some of you were aware of—the delicate yet penetrating vision Pope reveals—in that passage especially—the relationship of form to content, of content to form—a great tradition, no longer available to us who live now—to us who speak out of and to our era, and to no other—and—and—"

But the girl is shrieking with mirth. "*Pope!* Listen to *that*—*Pope!*" She is so excited, she has jumped up from her seat; her face is puffy, flushed, manic; she clasps her hands together and squeezes them between her knees, facing both you and the class, almost overcome with high spirits. Her shoulders are hunched, her forehead crinkled into innumerable furrows. And her mouth! Why had it seemed small? Her grin is cavernous—both rows of teeth show, glistening wet, and her warm moist gray-pink living tongue—it is naked, fascinating—horrible. You stare, you cannot look away. The entire class must be staring at the girl, unable to look away. "Hey! Wow! Did you get that, you guys?—he's testing you, tempting you! I heard of things like this—and of course his poetry revels in it—subtle ironies, complex propositions, odd jarring lapses of taste that must be intentional—holes in the imaginative vision that must be intentional—*must be*, since we're dealing with genius, eh?—and not ordinary folk! C'mon, hey, this class better *wake up*, or he's going to parody us all in his next poems!—where's your wit, your self-respect? There isn't any *vitality* in this class—I'm frankly shocked—the atmosphere reminds me of my silly sleepy high school classes—you guys just don't catch onto his subtlety, his ironic wisdom! The thing is, see, here's a recognized poetic genius testing us—like, if you guys thought that passage was by *Pope*—! Well, it sure as hell wasn't by Pope—it wasn't by anybody within a million miles of Pope—*Pope*, hah! See, he's testing us—playing a game with our complacencies—our middle-class aspirations and received opinions and fossilized metaphysical assumptions and—"

Your voice interrupts: "I will have to ask you to leave this class."

But no one hears; the girl does not hear. She is still talking, addressing the rest of the class, now waving her hands in wide circular patterns. You seize the chalk-tray behind you, your hands reaching instinctively back, backward, knowing you must stand firm, must not totter and fall. You are still speaking, you have not backed down: "—will have to ask you, miss, to leave this class, to leave this class. To leave this class. This class, now, this very moment, I will have to ask you to leave, I am asking you to leave, to *leave this class*," but no one hears, the girl is addressing the other girls exclusively now, Jan Holbien is actually smiling at her, a glazed but enthusiastic smile, and Rhoda Blair, sitting up quite straight in her seat, frowning, startled, seems to be intensely interested. The voice grows and grows in volume, yet has become more melodic, voluptuous and abrasive at the same time, wonderfully tantalizing:

"I mean—what I mean is—this is *genius! Genius!* You know what that means? Do you? The responsibility to one's art—the lifetime commitment—the priestly submergence of the individual self in the larger self—and, yes—yes—the occasional doubts—dreads—*angst* it was fashionably called in the Fifties—existential malaise paralleling the Dark Night of the Soul of a moribund Christianity—and yet, and yet!—the

descant

possibility of rebirth—resurrection—or at the very least some flights of manic joy—followed then by terrible depressions: the whole works, in other words. Do you see? Do you see? And here he stands—here, before us—in our presence—the visual physical form of the genius-poet—here, before us, in this commonplace setting! Too much, eh? Too much! Wild! He stands here, offers himself to us—to our constant judgment—the genius himself, the creature which Nietzsche said entire civilizations labor to produce—billions and trillions of dum-dums like you and me—just evolution—great masses of individuals—evolution laboring to produce a handful of geniuses—and you sit there on your rear-ends taking him for granted! God!—Okay, maybe the guy himself looks a little seedy—he's definitely aged since that photograph was taken—the famous one, the one that's been used so often—okay, sure, I grant you he's a lot shorter than one might expect—no more than 5'4", I'd estimate—and kind of squirrelly—his lips quivering like that, and a twitch in his left eye—and you can see (and almost smell!) the perspiration from where I stand—but—look—the thing is, the really great thing is, he's *real*. He's right here, he's still living and presumably still writing poetry, over the hill maybe—but maybe not—*mayyybeee not!*—don't forget old William Butler revving up when his spark-plugs kinda quit on him, and there's the handy example of Picasso too—no, no, you can't toss the first shovelful of dirt on this baby, he might have a few tricks left—he just might show everybody, his detractors especially —and us who sit in this very classroom today! The thing is, we don't want to let him down. And I accuse you guys of **letting him down**. I know I'm being extreme, but sometimes it's necessary: I accuse you guys of letting a genius down. Are you going to do anything about it? Are you going to change?—*change your lives?* Are you going to—"

A girl cries out: "Yes! I want to change my life!"

And another—it is Molly Brady herself, sweet Molly: "My God, yes! Yes! I want to change my life too! *Change my life!*"

Several girls join in; at the back of the room, Jocelyn Clark heaves herself to her feet and begins shouting. "Me! Me too! Don't leave me behind! Me! Me! *All of us!*"

"All of us!"
"ALL OF US!!"

You grow faint, totter, yet do not fall—you are holding onto the chalk-tray and cannot possibly fall—you are still smiling out at them, still in control. Their shouting and screaming and stamping rock the room, the girl in the green wool cap leads the chorus and is inching her way toward you, in time with the beat. Tears streak her plump cheeks, her moist muscular tongue appears and disappears and appears again, she is bouncing toward you in tiny rhythmic jumps, crying "All of us, yes dear God *all—all of us—all of us*–ALL!"

descant

D. C. Berry

The Garbage Man
—from *descant* 22.2 (Winter 1977)

        comes toting Tuesday,
hands swinging broken but matched
clockhands. Faces awry with Time.

    Pick up the garbage and stuff
it in the truck maw. Compress it with
a huge dirty truck lip—
    like that much snuff
in Joe Willie's jaw to spit.

    Drinks a beer when he gets home.
While I try to open Time,
fix the hands (make one longer
so they aren't matched) and faces.

Come Tuesday and I give it to Joe Willie.
He says Nope it wont do none
chews the long hand down
    and chunks the whole thing
into the truck maw.

And I compress my rage
with a Christian lip,
holding a curse full of juice
    in the bottom of my jaw,

D. C. Berry

look awry at the garbage can
and spit in my mouth
    (and my soul and guts)
at it,

open my booze
and drink till my hands are
uneven and my face

as full of time as a sun dial.

descant

Lee Abbott

Identify These Parts of the Body
—from *descant* 23.1 (Fall 1978)

for Ron K.

These come with caps and are often tricky
or knocked. Some have hair or pits and
scar tissue. An aging Pro Quarterback wears
expensive braces to support his. When a
gentleman places his hand on a lady's, it
usually means that he, too, is tricky. And
looking for support.

Frequently this is described as egg-shaped
or fat. In addition to gray matter, it
contains noodles, peas, and water. In the
desert, just before death, it sizzles
with visions.

Achilles had difficulty with this part
of his anatomy. Its vulnerability undid
him at a crucial pass in his life. Sometimes
it is confused with another feature of
interest, which is also unclean and unprotected
but virtually unheralded in the literature
of heroism.

Lee Abbott

Giraffes have long ones, women sensitive ones.
Men once believed both were exotic and
inaccessible. Southerners have popularized
the notion that it is rubber, red, or rough.
Usually, though, it is pale and stiff and
of uncertain geographic origin.

Katy Jurado's smoldered. Garbo covered hers
and many folks in Hollywood are still ashamed
of theirs. Typically, they flash and narrow
to slits. Once they conveyed the sentiments
of love, anger, resentment and joy. Years ago
they were said to resemble limpid pools and other
images drawn from nature. But it's been a long
time since one was spotted that wasn't red,
clouded or shamefully out of focus.

Jerry Bradley

Arrest
—from *descant* 22.4 (Summer 1978)

When they come for your first born
Remember that the phone book
Is full of family and lawyers,
That your little man will not rot
Because of the purse he stole,
The drugs he dealt.
Know too that looking into other
People's houses is not so bad,
Nor were the visits he made
And the things he removed.
The warrant just means someone noticed.
Perhaps he left a clue—
Your picture, his diploma,

Snot on a chair bottom—
Or confessed to what cannot be so.
No need to worry,
There are prayers stronger than lies
You can use when other appeals fail.
Mercy and revenge often go by other names,
Though their means much like justice are slow
As the caned steps of the elderly,
The beats of a reptilian heart,
Or celltime to a boy.

Tony Clark

Minor Accident Near the Check-out Stand
—from *descant* 25 (1980–81)

The sackboys started
At the shatter, then
Snickered, and a child
Bride in pink (an old
Man tried to cover
Up the jagged glass and
Applesauce with a blank
Stare) short-shorts glared
And said god, how sick;

But the old man
Was accustomed already
To dying (he put
A stiff gray hand
Into his pocket, feeling
Nothing but what
His thumb found,
And pulled out
Even change) piece by piece.

descant

Carol Coffee Reposa

Hill Country Rest Home
—from *descant* 28.1 (Winter-Fall 1983-84)

At the fort the flag flies all night long.
Inside the cold stone rooms
Are broken lanterns
Gusts of wind, Comanche arrows
Memories of spurs and flint
Dingy photographs of Johnston, Thomas, Lee
Behind cracked glass.

From this rise a visitor sees everything:
The tired kaleidoscope
Of storefronts faced in river rock
Tile rooftops, stunted trees
And lines of slowly moving cars.

Beyond the hills
I hear the muffled roar
Of cannon, underbrush snapped
By rag-wrapped, bleeding feet
In quick retreat
A tattered blanket
Thrown across the back
Dead dreams ripping at the brain.

Carol Coffee Reposa

Below are rusty pickups
Tidy hospitals
Retirement homes to house the ghosts
Of other wars
While somewhere
Just before the morning medication
After all the doors are locked
The General surrenders
To the yuccas and bluebonnets,
Scores of wrinkled soldiers
Hobbling on to Appomattox.

descant

Taylor Graham

Bottles
—from *descant* 31.2 (Spring–Summer 1987)

           Scraping
to get the label off. Never know
what you'll find inside:
boat made of matchsticks,
message floated across
these stormy blocks of city
to him shipwrecked. A bird.
Lacking cages, people slipped
songbirds down bottle-throats
safe-keeping till the wind
came down.

Songbird! Bones left
thinner than toothpicks.

What else in bottles? Ends
of perfume, something to sell.
        Sniff. The bones
of the grape, a red glass
to look through
for sunset.

Larry D. Thomas

Herefords in Winter
—from *descant* 32.2 (1988)

It's nine degrees above zero.
They stand still in the pasture, staring
at nothing but the barbs of taut wire,

the sky above them so blue and cold
that even the hawks have taken shelter.
They stare chewing their cud

against a distant backdrop of cap rock
their white faces hover over
like full, haunting moons familiar with sky

and the feeble daily scaldings
of the sun. They stare straight through
their barbed and lone existences,

surviving the cold,
flourishing in their heaven
of bleakness.

DESCANT

FORT WORTH'S JOURNAL OF POETRY AND FICTION

Fall 1998　　　　　　　　　　　Vol. 38.2

1990-2005

꧁ Introduction

From 1990 through 2005, the journal experienced rapid changes in editorship compared to the consistency of the prior decades. In the early 1990s, Betsy Colquitt, Harry Opperman, Steve Sherwood, and Stanley Trachtenberg served as joint editors. After Colquitt's retirement, Neil Easterbrook, Sherwood, and Trachtenberg edited the journal, and in 1997 and 1998, Easterbrook and managing editors Billie Hara and Joel Causey produced the issues. In 1999, David Kuhne co-edited with Easterbrook and then became principal editor in 2000. This was also the year that saw *descant* become an annual publication. Kuhne, who is associate director of the TCU Center for Writing, received an MFA from the University of Arkansas and a Ph.D. from TCU. He continues to serve as current editor of the journal. Lynn Risser, a retired English professor who holds a Ph.D. from the University of Arkansas and whose work has appeared in volumes such as the *Oxford Companion to Twentieth-Century Poetry*, has been the poetry editor of the journal since 2001. While the volumes from these years no doubt reflect the editors' strengths and interests, the quality and tenor of the journal remained seamless throughout the many transitions of the 1990s. Since Kuhne became editor, the journal has added three annual awards, in addition to the Frank O'Connor Award instituted in 1978: The Colquitt Award, the Baskerville Publisher's Award, and the Gary Wilson Award. The generosity of these awards, the reputation of *descant*, and publishing opportunities for new writers contribute to what has also been an unprecedented number of submissions to the journal since the turn of the century. While *descant* has always been a venue seeking to foster the talents of newer writers (Hadara Bar-Nadav, Catherine McCraw, John Perryman, Mark Wagenaar, and many more), it continues to publish such established voices as Jonis Agee, Denise Duhamel, Clyde Edgerton, William Harrison, Rita Ann Higgins, and Virgil Suarez.

Kuhne, who knows well the history and literary rhythms of the journal, adhered to its traits of being a national journal that also highlights work of Southwest and Texas authors, as pieces in this anthology from William Harrison ("Dove Season") and Bruce Machart ("Where You Begin") indicate. In order to celebrate the rich offerings of Texas writers, in fact, the 2000 issue of *descant* was a special Texas Writers issue guest edited by acclaimed novelist Clay Reynolds. Contributors to the Texas Writers issue who also appear in this volume include such authors as Clyde Edgerton, R.S. Gwynn, Annette Sanford, and Andrew Hudgins.

Moreover, since 2001, when Mary Volcansek became dean of TCU's Addran College of Humanities and Social Sciences, *descant* has had secure funding, something many small journals do not have. *descant* quietly and continually receives critical acclaim. Newpages.com, a resource for independent bookstores, publishers, literary journals, and readers, writes that *descant* is "a slim, fine volume, an annual that, once you know it, is something to look forward to like the longest day of summer and cool nights thereafter." *Small Magazine Review* also raves about *descant*, saying "*descant* may be the best kept secret of Fort Worth, Texas. It is a must read." Bruce Machart's "Where you Begin" has been anthologized by *Texas Bound*, and Annette Sanford's "Nobody Listens When I Talk," first appearing in *descant* in 1976 and reprinted in the Texas Writers issue, was chosen by Barbara Kingsolver for inclusion in *Best American Short Stories 2001*.

The writers in this final section of the *descant* retrospective, some mentioned above, exemplify the many layers that make *descant* distinctive and one of the few literary journals still in continuous production for so long, offering poetry and prose from local, regional, and national writers at various stages of their writing careers, writers whose works can juxtapose clean and messy, or subtle and shocking, while always retaining a deftness and richness that leaves readers eagerly awaiting the next volume.

—Charlotte Hogg

Ulf Kirchdorfer

Fish
—from *descant* 34.1 (1990)

As a boy I dreamed of standing
in the middle of our farm pond
holding my mother's sewing hoop
just above the surface.

Little fish jumped, doing their
friendly tricks and talking
to me. We spoke of the water
temperature and school.

When I later baited a hook
and set it in the fish's
cartilage mouth, that was fine
too.

Robert Wexelblatt

We Lead Three Lives
—from *descant* 35.1 (1995)

Elsewhere it's true nature never leaps and
nothing comes from nothing only down here
utopias can spurt ex nihilo
from a cornucopia and divers
insisting on their right to gravity
will splashlessly land where we have dreamt
up pool or lake thus making is not is
with unhobbled playfulness juggling all
four elements to suit our desires
elusive nymph and tree salesman and bug
we shuffle physics with fatality
bent on meaning and gaiety of heart

Lucidity that is as good as French
relished while reclining on a bench
idly teasing pigeons, toting up the crowd
parading primly by, is never loud
or argumentative, each small insight
an aperçu whispered to the twilight,
for this world's poison the sovereign serum
pure as the Pythagorean Theorem
proving itself. A trim neo-cortex
is fit for calculus though not for sex,
a let-there-be dividing light from dark,
the music from the motions of the park.

Robert Wexelblatt

Down below the routine pyrotechnics
of climbing in and out of queen-sized beds,
out and into jeans, life ticktocks with the
apatheia of a Stoic's heart, the
stupid detachment of a bomb that while
we are otherwise engaged may strew
archetypes across two intersections,
three counties, one green desk blotter. With Love
and Strife unreconciled Empedocles
dove into Aetna's fire; so bubbles and froths
the subcutaneous life where dreams are
forged, hammer strokes to shatter all our plans.

descant

Robert Coles

In Sweden
—from *descant* 36.2 (1996)

We had just left Marsalla
when we passed
underneath a bridge,
large letters scrawled in white:

NO NIGGERS.

I sat up in my seat,
the train speeding
towards Sweden's ancient capital.
My knuckles bent into fists;
even here I could not escape
the color of my skin.

In the afternoon,
I climbed the hill that led to the castle,
where Queen Christina quit the throne
because she did not love war.
Now children played among
the rusting cannons.
When I came down
at the end of the day,
I stopped in a cafe to rest.
Through the windows
I watched a black man
helping a blind man
who didn't seem to mind,
nor did the people who crossed the street.

Robert Parham

Hurricane
—from *descant* 37.1 (Spring 1997)

At four, the gray Atlantic's raucous curl
surged heavy up the boulevard, the spit
of transformers spending ozone in the mist.

The Guard backs jeeps along the waterline,
their nervous cheer seals junctures where drunk surfers
beg to go into that quintessential rush.

Decrepit, with his dog, an old salt slumps
from houses thought deserted. He holds the mutt
and scruffs his grizzled beard against its coat.

A dryer and a washer bob along the street,
windows pop and doors push out, whole houses
rise and drift southward down the shore, a boat

without a manifest, no sail, no destination
made, as all bad promises, in shallow depths.

Jill Patterson

Any Minute
—from *descant* 37.2-38.1 (Fall 1997-Spring 1998)

Our car jerks into the fast lane. You're speeding, driving 80 in a 65. Any minute, we might round a corner and smash into a crawling line of afternoon traffic. When I remind you my mother is lagging behind us, refusing to break the limit, you don't even check the speedometer.

"My father used to say women become their mothers. *Always meet the girl's mother,* he said." You grin like you've cracked a joke.
But you know I'm dreading my mother's visit. It's her first since we moved in together; she's neurotic, and there's no telling what devastation she's brought with her. Ignoring my silence, you start a conversation with the radio. Your timing is perfect: you ask old Garth when he'll lie down and quit, just before he answers, *Ain't going down 'til the sun comes up, ain't giving in 'til we get enough.*

Suddenly, a woman rips into the middle lane. Her Pinto slams into the slot beside our car then matches our pace. She waves and honks her horn—two beeps then one sustained wail. Her jaw hangs in an open grimace as if she's eaten a bite of food that's too hot to swallow. When I roll down my window, she screams, "Go home! Lock your doors! Armageddon starts tonight at 10:15!" Icy and solid as steelies, her eyes stare at me. Then she gives her engine the gun. As she shoots ahead, I see several bags of groceries crammed in her back seat, supplies for the upcoming crisis. You point out the bumper sticker: *He is Coming Soon.*

I yank down the vanity mirror and spot my mother's car in the traffic behind us.

You lean forward and punch your favorite radio station. "She can't blame you for the Second Coming."

"Very funny." I shut off the radio. Of course, I can't prevent every city crack-up from colliding with my mother, but does a deranged zealot have to run her off the road? Isn't it enough my mother has descended from Oklahoma to pass judgment on our live-in status? No doubt she'll argue that crazy woman proves that living in a big city can batter one's mind or morals, drive anybody—even me—to move in with rather than marry a man.

And yet—the eerie thing about some loony predicting the imminent end of the world, from behind the wheel of her fiery Pinto during Dallas rush-hour—is how she belongs there. She blends with the gangs, drive-by shootings, and car-jackings. The traffic, tilting in unison around the curves and overpasses, is cocked with the same anger I saw in her marbled eyes. What if a single mad car swerved into another lane, provoked another driver? Would it trigger the end?

I twist around in my seat. A Cadillac and a Ryder van cut off my mother's car from ours. "I should have ridden with her."

"She insisted," you say.

And she had insisted. Lately she'd decided to expand her comfort zone. She was starting with automobiles: learning to gas up her car instead of letting my father do it, reading maps for herself, and maneuvering the six lane freeways in Dallas. Caught in the fury of the five o'clock current, she had missed her exit then drove for twenty more minutes before calling. When we met her at the Friendship Mart, her eyes tightened into rocks. Angry as well as afraid, she refused to let me ride with her, said she wasn't so stupid she couldn't *follow* a car without help.

"Maybe that woman didn't warn your mother," you offer. "Maybe your mother's not one of the chosen. She doesn't have a flag on her car."

I laugh though you're not trying to be funny now. You're upset that I didn't tell my mother *No* when she suggested we tie her red scarf to our antennae so she could sight us more easily. The breeze snatches the silk, a taut warning. It doesn't seem like a noticeable thing, though other drivers stare. They're wondering if we're heading up a funeral, promoting AIDS awareness, or demonstrating patriotism for some militia group.

descant

"Be glad you're not the president," I say. "Then you'd have tiny American flags waving all over your car."

Up ahead, the traffic lurches. Brake lights stagger then pop on. Red hot impatience. You punch the brakes seconds before we ram an eighteen-wheeler. "My brother quit his job once," you say. "Moved to Arizona and lived in a tent for ten months. Some minister convinced him the end was coming. At the Grand Canyon. He cooked on a portable Coleman. Waiting. For ten months." You release the wheel and hold up your hands. All ten fingers wiggle.

This is one of those moments I fear will remain after our relationship collapses. When it comes time to pinpoint the first sign of trouble, I'll remember how my mother's blood-red hankie annoyed you, how you wove our car in and out of the faster lanes as if trying to ditch her, and how, wiggling your fingers, you smiled too big, miming happiness.

Outside, the red scarf ripples then snaps tight. The digital clock on the dash reads 5:35. I want to ask if you, too, feel the end lurking in the rearview mirror, tailing us until the appointed hour and place. You must be taking that woman's prediction somewhat seriously, or you wouldn't mention your brother and the Grand Canyon.

I bow my head, peering in the side-view mirror to make sure mother is still there. "Don't tell her that story about the Grand Canyon," I say.

The traffic simmers. A distant siren strains. I tell myself I'm being silly. When 10:15 rolls around, I'll be in a place too frantic to feel the floor drop from beneath me, form a final, cavernous hole. In the frenzy of other things, does anyone notice prophesies coming true? Remembering that woman's back seat full of groceries, I'm already thinking he forgot to buy coffee for my mother, and she'll want a cup first thing in the morning.

My mother walks into our apartment, sets down her overnight bag, and marches to the couch where she shuffles the toss pillows into a more balanced design. Then she adjusts the pictures on the wall and moves the rocker to the window where a person can get some light if he wishes to sit and read. You cock your head and smirk, behind my mother's back. You understand what I meant about her uncontrollable urges to tidy up after me. "That's great," you say. My mother thinks you're referring to the new pillow arrangement and answers, "You're welcome."

She picks up her bag and heads for the guest room where she'll organize our storage closet, check for fresh mothballs, then unpack her own clothes and hang them up. Maybe we can interpret her willingness to rearrange our household as a sign she accepts your apartment, feels comfortable fixing it. You put one arm around my waist and grab my chin with your free hand like you do sometimes before you kiss me. Then you change your mind. "Guess she didn't see the prophet lady on the freeway."

I kiss you anyway, because I've already puckered my lips. You're talking when my lips touch yours, and it feels funny kissing a mouth doing something else. We laugh. Missing one another like this is an intimate moment now, but later I'll wonder if this confusion didn't signify faulty communication.

At dinner, my mother says she doesn't believe it's possible to predict the end of the world or the end of anything for that matter. "Take that woman driving on the highway. Practically causing a car wreck." She puts down her fork, waiting while she chews a bite of steak. "You see her?" she asks.

All I can do is nod my head.

"She was crazy," my mother continues. "You can't predict the end like that. It's going to come—bang!" She slams her palm on the table. "No warning. No nothing." She gets up and walks around the table to refill your tea glass, looks at mine and sees I have plenty, then returns to her seat. "You know, I woke up one night, and your father wasn't in bed. The dark crowded me. I felt sweaty from all the night-fears you imagine. I kept waiting for him, watching the digital clock blink away the minutes. Then it occurred to me: *It's Armageddon and the Good Lord botched it/ He took that scamp of a husband and left me behind/*" She shakes her head. "Course, I found your father reading in the bathroom and realized how silly I'd been. But it's going to happen like that. People won't hear anything. Half the population will just be gone."

descant

You agree. Half the population isn't awake now, so why wouldn't they sleep through the end?

My mother lifts her head, watches you cut your steak. You don't look up. Her brow wrinkles, and though she still stares at you, I see her mind swerve into one of those empty gazes blind people use because they've never learned how to direct their vision. "Sometimes people up and leave," she says. "Disappear. Like the end of the world, but smaller. Sometimes a woman doesn't see it coming."

I understand: she means you, not having married me, might skip town any day. I hold my breath. The meat I've swallowed lodges above my Adam's apple, a tight knot.

You cut your steak in neat squares, graciously ignoring what she's said. Or so I think. "My brother," you start, "waited for the Second Coming at the Grand Canyon. Waited for ten months."

I'm about to take a bite of carrot. Instead, I leave my fork suspended in front of my mouth. My stopping in mid-action is meant to remind you, although I see you remember perfectly well you weren't supposed to tell my mother that story. Your head tilts, and you smirk, this time not caring that my mother notices. You wear this smug face often—like when you whip me at Scrabble though we both know you cheated, using pronouns, foreign phrases, misspelled words. You mean to say you recognize—but won't tolerate—anyone's urges to straighten your lifestyle.

Your attempts to shock my mother onto some topic other than our lack of a marriage certificate fail. "Dallas isn't a safe place to raise children, either," she adds.

My fork clatters onto my plate. I can't believe we're having this conversation.

"It's not," she insists.

"And you know," you say, "we'd like to start a family. Maybe have a go tonight." You squeeze my elbow, grinning. You've been dying to tell either one of my parents that, in case there's any doubt, we are having sex. I pull my mouth into a crooked line that says *Real cute*. "I'd like a boy," you continue. "We could move to Big Piney, Wyoming, name him Bob Wire or John Wayne."

"Stop kidding her," I say.

My mother giggles, nervous. She hopes it's the sex part, not the names *Bob Wire* or *John Wayne,* you're joking about. The three of us wait. The air seems emptied of anything to breathe but car exhaust, as if the traffic from this afternoon has driven into our house and sits, idling.

Later, when I'm doing the dishes and you've gone to buy coffee, my mother comes into the kitchen, raises her hands—palms outward—like little stop signs. She rests them on my shoulders. "Not that it's any of my business," she begins, "but we don't know him. He could have diseases."

My initial reaction is to ask if *know* means *know* like in the Biblical sense. "We know all about protection," I say instead. I don't mean to be flip, because, of course, I do worry about diseases.

"Just checking." She puts one hand to her mouth and turns it like she's twisting a key. "Tick a lock." She walks out of the kitchen only to swish right back in before the door swings shut. "He's not a homosexual or anything, is he?" she asks. "I mean, you need protection, don't you?"

"Mother." I shake my head.

"Okay, okay," she says, waving her hands, erasing our conversation.

She doesn't leave the kitchen though. She stands there, watching me wash dishes like she watched you cut your steak. When I look up to acknowledge her, her bottom lip trembles. Her whole mouth crumples, curls from crying but trying not to. She tells me she's afraid of everything. She hasn't meant to impact me, but she hears my voice cut out when I talk about marriage and divorce—collisions and smashups.

I know this is one of those sad images I'll remember. When it comes time to recall my mother, say after she's dead and I need something solid to clutch, I'll remember how embarrassed she was when she set off a fire extinguisher in the car, or how her legs snapped the wrong direction after a ski accident, or how her lips quivered when she stood in my kitchen and cried because she felt responsible for all my fears.

I place a clean, dripping saucer in her left hand and a towel in the right. The only thing she can do for me, at this point, is help dry my dishes. "One thing I've learned, Mother," I say, turning back to my soapy water, "maybe I'll always fear the end: Maybe I can't predict it. But I hope I'm awake when it happens."

I look at the clock. It's a quarter after eight—8:18 p.m. to be exact. We've less than two hours to go. I wish you would hurry and return from the grocery with my mother's coffee. A steaming cup of Folger's Mountain Grown might be soothing in the final moments.

After my mother goes to bed early and we're undressing in the bathroom, you move behind me and kiss my shoulder where the skin dips over the collar bone. "How about a late night drive? It'll relax you."

My father used to tell my mother a hot bath would relax her. I smile. I love riding in cars, speeding through the dark, windows down, heading nowhere, the six freeway lanes open. I press my cheek to your chin. Something about you whispering right in my ear seems familiar.

When I suggest we leave a note for my mother, you tease me but are more annoyed than amused. I insist. So I'm grateful you suggest driving all the way around Loop 635. Maybe a long ride will soften the anger that's been swelling all afternoon. Our car glides around the curves, slides from lane to lane. I crack my window. The evening air spills inside. For this one hour, nothing—nothing—seems threatening. My head falls against the seat. My breathing relaxes, stretches a full yawn.

I turn in my seat, extend my legs across your lap, and run one toe along the in-seam of your jeans, up your thigh. You wiggle your eyebrows but don't move to caress my legs. You're concentrating on the road. My working so hard to distract you always makes you want to get home quicker and stop fooling around in the car. This is one of the things I hope you'll remember, one thing you'll tell your next girlfriend about, if she's afraid of any carry-overs—emotional diseases—you might bring with you.

I try to remember something cheerful about your ex-girlfriend Katie. All you've said is how close you came to getting married. The date was set, the bridesmaids and groomsmen picked, and that endless white dress bought, altered, and hanging from the curtain rod in Katie's bedroom where everyone had come to admire it. Though you describe it nonchalantly, I can tell from the way you become quiet afterward, the thing you remember most is the night she told you she couldn't through with it.

It's the way she knocked on your front door at three in the morning, the way your roommate heard it and you didn't, the way he let her into your room and she woke you whispering, *Rick, we need to talk*. More than anything else, it's how that application from Visa arrived three months later, addressed to *Mrs. Katie Sullivan*, her first name coupled with your last, because somebody, somewhere didn't know it had all been canceled.

"You remember anything good about Katie?" I ask.

Your head jerks. You're wondering why I'm suddenly asking about your ex-girlfriend. "About Kat? You don't need to worry about her." You think I'm feeling jealous, really want to hear how she didn't shave often enough, stole the covers at night, or made you buy feminine products at the grocery store. Little do you know that what I want is proof you're alive—not broken down with fear.

I'm not worried," I say. "I want to know if you remember anything good."

"She never believed me when I told her I loved her." You stare straight ahead, silent, accusing.

"She doubted you? That's something good?" I wait for a moment. "You nicknamed her. *Kat for Katie*. That's sweet."

"Your name's already short. How can I change *Beth*?"

I shake my head. "Forget it."

"Big deal," you say. "You can't remember anything good about Mark."

You're wrong, but I don't say so. I'm unpacking my memories slowly. Having thought they included nothing more than the pain of farewell, I'd stored them like throw-away clothes. The memories may be wrinkled and faded, but I enjoy trying them on. "He used to whisper in my ear. Right in my ear."

"That's it? He whispered in your ear?"

descant

I try a different tactic. "He loved my lingerie," I say. "My baby blue lingerie."

You look at me, full in the face, for the first time since we got in the car. "I've never seen your blue lingerie."

You tilt your attention back toward the road. I admit I'm feeling guilty. Guilty—because I'm not telling you how people stared at Mark and the plastic tubes threading into his nose when he began needing oxygen everyday, how he almost ran out one afternoon before we could get him to the hospital for another tank, and how that day shook me so roughly, we knew, when I walked out the door that night, I wasn't coming back. My mother congratulated me the next morning, gave me a sturdy hug. "You're learning," she said. "What else could you do? You can't fall in love with death." She patted my leg. She must have thought I'd finally learned to drive defensively.

Clyde Edgerton

Out of Rosehaven
—from *descant* 39.1–39.2 (Spring–Fall 2000)

Today, Aunt Lil's got on her green striped jacked over her pink sweat suit. She's wearing a yellow scarf and heavy make-up. And diapers, now. I'm driving Mama's Chevrolet and twice Aunt Lil thinks it's her car.

At her apartment—which we're still keeping for the time being—I open the mailbox. It's stuffed, mostly junk mail, three bunches with rubber bands, several "Have You Seen Me?" flyers. And what the banks of America are doing to the mailboxes of America is a shame on every one of us. The money Citibank has spent on mail could buy 2000 nursing homes.

"Let's see," I say, "there are a couple of get-well cards in here, it looks like, and your bank account, and then mostly junk. Let's go upstairs."

I follow two steps below her, bringing up her walker. She is very slowly climbing the stairs. She holds to the rail. Until her fall she always took one step at a time.

"See, I can do this all right," she says.

"Yes ma'am, you can. That's good." Aunt Lil, you wouldn't last five minutes by yourself.

Up top, I put her walker in front of her and at the door she asks, "Is that the right key?"

"Yes ma'am." No, it's the wrong key. I thought I'd try a few wrong ones first.

I follow her in through the door. Inside is her big soft couch with wooden arms, coffee table, a big chair, a desk, her TV facing a chair with small squares of cut carpet placed around it—for dropped ashes. On the wall over the couch is a large framed print of the old Summerlin Courthouse. For some reason she loves that thing. A reprint of a painting of red cherries in a bowl hangs on the dining area

descant

wall beside a certificate, Lillian W. Olive, Burrough's Business School. Beneath the cherries and certificate is a small table with family photographs. Most all of us in one picture or another.

I drop the mail on the dining room table, go back over to the couch, sit down, look around. I don't have much time.

"I can get around without this walker in here. Don't you think so?"

"I think that would work all right. Keep a hand on something."

"I just want to look around."

She touches the back of a living room chair, then holds to it, slowly moves and reaches to her TV chair, to the back of a dining room chair. She slowly and carefully sits at the dining room table. She picks up one of her cigarette lighters and looks at it, puts it back down, picks up another one. She looks all around. She picks up a pepper shaker with "Washington D.C." on it. Our Nation's Capital.

"Cigarette lighters," she says. "That picture of them cherries."

"You said something about some more shoes," I say. "Do you want to check and see if there are some more shoes you want to take in?"

"Oh, yes, shoes. I want to see if I've still got those bedroom shoes with the hard rubber bottoms. Something that won't be so slick."

She stands, looks into the kitchen. The pantry door was left open—I can see canned string beans and other canned goods shelved very neatly, a stack of paper bags, a broom and dustpan.

"I don't see why I can't come back here. Do you?"

"Well, I . . . no. We just need to try it a little longer. You know what the doctor said."

"I don't like him. Do you?"

"Well, I don't know," I tell her. "It's hard to find a good one nowadays."

When I take her in, her doctor talks to me with her sitting there—talks to me like she might be four months old. A lot of people do that. You can't change that.

"Would you shut that pantry door?" she says.

"Yes ma'am." I look inside the pantry, wonder about all those canned goods, shut the door, find Aunt Lil in the hall, and there is her waist-high book case holding her three dictionaries, a few other books, a history of Hansen County, three small bowls, a copy of *Out of Africa* which I remember has a cut out space—about the size and shape of a pack of cigarettes—inside. Uncle Carl hid money in there when he came back from World War II. I once tried to get her to talk about Uncle Carl, but she kept changing the subject, so I gave up.

"You go up to the doctor's office," says Aunt Lil, "and you don't know who you're going to see. . . . Let's check on them shoes. Oh, look. My dictionaries. Let's get a dictionary. And I want to see my Kirby. It's still in the bedroom, idn't it?"

"It's still in there." She'd rather me die than that Kirby.

"Let's get your walker," I say. "We can't be too careful. Stop right there."

I get the walker from the living room, and returning, I can see straight over her head. I remember—when I was little—wrestling with her every year at the saw mill, when we'd go there to get mulch for her and Mama's flowers, and I'd get around behind her and reach up and grab her shoulders, hold on and ride her down to the ground. Mama would be sitting in the bed of the pick-up, like the mama in *Cool Hand Luke*.

Aunt Lil let me drive her Plymouth Fury to my senior prom. She was my wildest aunt, and laughed the longest and hardest.

First room on the left in the hall is the extra bedroom, mostly empty. In the corner stands that 1963 Kirby vacuum cleaner—famous because she's bought two new ones since buying that one, but returned both and each time repossessed the '63. There's a table lamp on the floor, and a rolled up rug. On the closet shelf she's got several rolls of toilet paper, six bottles of Jergen's lotion, three jars of Pond's cold cream, and all her vacuum cleaner implements.

Next room down the hall is the bathroom. In the tub is where she fell, and then when she was getting up, fell again.

At the end of the hall is the bedroom. Three-piece bedroom suite, dark wood, many pairs of shoes over by her dresser.

Walk-in closet. Clothes hanging. Small metal file box on the floor. Among the other papers is her will. She got me to go through it all with her.

On the wall is a photograph of her and the other girls in her business school class, standing on the steps of the school, smiling, waving like they're on the cover of *Look* magazine.

"I don't see any reason at all I shouldn't come on back home," she says.

What I see in my head is this apartment empty and me sitting on the floor with my back against the wall, having moved everything out. I don't look forward to that. I check my watch.

"I probably need to be getting on pretty soon," I say.

She touches her TV chair. "Can I just sit in the living room another few minutes."

"Sure."

We sit for awhile, and later, going down the steps, she stops. I'm in front of her, so I stop and turn to look—her up there above me, stooped, a piece of diaper showing at her waist where she or the aide or somebody tucked her blouse into it.

"Why are you in such a hurry?" she says. She's frowning.

"I'm not in a hurry," I say. "I've just got a few things to do."

"I used to come home. Now I visit home. I appreciate you helping me out."

"You're welcome. I'm glad to do it."

"I hope you have somebody. I hope you're as lucky as I am when you get in such a fix. I hope you have somebody to save your home for you, even if it's just an apartment."

I stand there and take that in and try to move my mind on forward to such a time. And then we get on out to the parking lot, load up, and head back to Rosehaven.

R. S. Gwynn

The Porch Swing
–from *descant* 39.1-39.2 (Spring-Fall 2000)

After a photograph by Russell Lee, 1941

    In the new moon's light she might be taken
    For darker than she is. Perhaps she'll sing
    A spiritual. Her young son sleeps, unshaken
    By troubles that the R.F.D. may bring
    This morning to the leaning rusted box.
    Till then, there is a moment: she is free
    To range beyond a world of bars and locks.
    His book lies open: Possibility.

    Listen. Isn't the steady creaking of the chain
    Comfort enough against the breaking dark?
    If her small motions make the only sound,
    Then it is she, for once, who can contain
    This world, secured and measured by the arc
    Of feet that do not have to touch the ground.

descant

Andrew Hudgins

Flamingos Have Arrived in Ashtabula
—from *descant* 39.1–39.2 (Spring–Fall 2000)

Flamingos have arrived in Ashtabula.
Or one has. Bending to fetch the morning paper,
the mayor saw it standing on her lawn,
poised one-legged like a plastic bird
jabbed in the grass, and thinking it a joke,
she laughed. It lumbered, lurched into the air
and sailed across her back fence, rising pink
against the near-pink Ashtabula dawn.

Flamingos have arrived in Ashtabula,
blown here we think by a line of thunderstorms
—a scrap of pink confetti on the wind—
except those storms were months ago. Escaped
from a zoo, we speculate, though doubtfully.
No zoo nearby reports a lost flamingo.
It doesn't seem lost. It circles the airport tower,
lands from time to time on the firehouse roof,
and stabs frogs in the mudhole back of Wal-Mart,
where people linger with binoculars
to watch a flamingo feed in Ashtabula.

Andrew Hudgins

A local bar, once Dewey's Hometown Lounge,
has changed to The Pink Flamingo. On Saturdays,
it throws flamingo parties—pink drinks and pink
Bermuda shorts on all the waitresses.
Stuck in the ceiling, hundreds of plastic pink
flamingos hang over us upside down, observing,
while we sip pink gin and ponder the waitress'
tight pink tee-shirts. From them, even pinker pink
flamingos with sequin eyes return our gaze.
Flamingos have arrived in Ashtabula.

The tropical bodies resplendent against gray sky,
the languid beating of long wings—we see them clearly
in our imagining and dreams, and now
in daylight we scan the sky expectantly
and check each bog and wallow near the road
for a hint of pink or parrot-green, a red
that shimmers. Turquoise. Electric yellow eyes.
Or I do. I speak for no one but myself.
Flamingos have arrived in Ashtabula.

William Harrison

Dove Season
—from *descant* 40 (Spring-Fall 2001)

The old man hassled his son all morning, complaining that the coffee wasn't strong enough, that one of the shotguns had been removed from its case too early so that morning dew settled on it, and that the kid's grades—he had finished a year at the local college—had better improve.

"Once mediocre, always mediocre," the old man snapped at him, and his son grew sullen as they started walking the path at the edge of the farm. The old man, Cobb Yoder, was now almost seventy years old. He had driven off his two older sons, so now only Jackdog, nineteen years old and the son of Cobb's second wife, was left to hunt with him.

"Try to get through the day," the old man went on. "Don't step on no rattlesnakes and don't be makin' any fancy swing shots so I get in the line of fire."

"Don't worry, I won't shoot you," Jackdog answered.

"What's that?"

"Nothing. Mind the culvert."

They went into a culvert, then climbed out, going along that edge of the farm that fronted the grey waters of Baffin Bay.

"And slow down, dammit," the old man protested.

By this time Jackdog seethed with anger, but kept silent.

They went another hundred yards, stepping over an old coil of barbed wire and crossing a patch of weeds, but no birds flew up.

"I bet you miss football season," Cobb said, making a first feeble attempt at real conversation.

"Not a bit," Jackdog answered, and he knew well enough why his father mentioned it. After all, it was only six man football played on a dusty field up at the Riviera Beach school, but it gave the old man an opportunity, after years of having no sons to watch at the local games, to sit in the stands and brag with his drinking buddies. For a minute Jackdog remembered the games, the girls, and the camaraderie with the Garza boys and others, but he didn't miss it.

"You just won't say, but you liked football," the old man persisted.

"No, because when I played linebacker I never hit hard enough and when I played fullback I never ran far enough to suit you," Jackdog told him. "So I don't miss it one goddamned bit."

That ended that.

The complaints started again when Cobb said, "I notice you didn't shake out your boots this morning. You could've stuck your foot right down on a scorpion."

Jackdog just kept on walking.

When the sun came up they opened the thermos and drank the coffee Jackdog had made, eating a wedge of cheese with it.

"Where in hell are all the birds?" the old man asked the sky.

Jackdog knew how to keep quiet and irritate his father, so did.

After finishing his coffee, Cobb said, "Okay, we'll turn inland. We'll hunt them two long fence rows, c'mon."

"I'll stay along the beach," Jackdog replied.

"What for? Ain't no birds here."

"I'll take my chances."

"If you didn't want to hunt today, you should've said so."

Cobb could hunt alone, Jackdog told himself; and once again he let the silence stand between them until finally he added, "Meet you back at the shack at lunch time. We'll see who found the birds and who didn't."

"All right then," his father said with an angry snort, and he thrust the empty thermos back into Jackdog's hands and stalked off.

Walking alone, Jackdog's anger ebbed away. The midday heat of September hadn't yet started and he enjoyed shaking out his aching limbs, having slept in a bedroll in the yard outside the shack where, once, long ago, his grandfather had lived out his last days. Exiled to the far end of the Yoder farm, his grandfather: a three room shack, useless now, with a rickety dock that stuck out sixty feet into the waters of the bay. He never really knew old Jack Yoder, but his mother told him stories: a leathery old man, alone, playing solitaire, fishing for drum and less than edible fish, coming up to the big house on Sundays for supper.

descant

A dove flew up, but far out of range.

Loyola Beach lay to the east of Baffin Bay, a salty shallows between Padre Island and the South Texas mainland. Every springtime rattlesnakes floated across the briny waters, coming ashore at Loyola to occupy a thorny countryside of mesquite trees, nettles, cactus, yucca, lizards and scorpions. Along the beach sad driftwood and the rotted carcasses of fish gathered in a residue of oil, smelly seaweed, bottlecaps, defecation, and slime. Where the road ended at the boat ramp the ramshackle Fisherman's Inn stood perched on pilings, serving everything fried: shrimp, filets, potatoes, oysters, hush puppies, and Mexican beans. On the weathered dock a few misguided fishermen sometimes pulled their faded boats up to the rusted pumps. The old man loved the Inn and all his beer drinking buddies inside it, all of them content to gather in a place as grim as the landscape itself.

Just north of the Inn the Yoder land started: more than a thousand acres hacked out of a prickly terrain by Grandfather Jack, his son Cobb, and Cobb's sons and given over to cotton farming. When the earth was turned over for the fall planting thousands of doves arrived and for a few days the Yoders and their farm workers, especially the large Garza family, enjoyed the shooting.

Two birds, flushed out as Cobb went along the fence row, flew with the strong southern breeze so that Jackdog, giving them a big lead, brought them down. Two good quick shots. He started across the soft field to pick them up.

"Dogs! We need ourselves some dogs!" he said aloud as he made his way over the furrows. That was another thing to be angry about, having no dogs. They had Beau and Spirit, once, but Cobb neglected them and when they finally died the old man offered the opinion that a good wing shot didn't really need a retriever in the month of September when the ground lay so bare.

Jackdog circled the field, found the birds and placed them in his pouch. After walking back to the path beside the beach, lifting his boots high over the furrows, he was sweaty and pissed off again.

The sorry, mean-spirited, stingy, stubborn, dumb son of a bitch:

he had recently raised a hand against Jackdog's mother again after all the promises that it wouldn't happen another time. The argument: a pair of shoes she had bought for him, a pair he claimed he didn't need. In spite of himself, Jackdog went down a list. No dogs. Farm equipment in lousy shape. The Garzas constantly and rightfully angry, so that Tony finally quit in disgust, went off, and joined the army. Beer and bullshit every night at the Inn. Something had to be done.

Suddenly the birds came up.

They came from the fence rows by the dozens, sailing on rising breeze, heading from his left to right so fast that he could only shoot, load, and shoot again. From downwind they came and kept coming in a long rope of frantic wings. Swinging his gun, giving them a big lead, he pulled off shot after shot, at war with the whole dove population of South Texas, it seemed, missing dozens while stopping to reload. One, two, a double: he never missed. The old Stevens felt wonderful as it warmed in his hands. He himself felt oiled and ready as if he had waited all his hunting years—since he was nine years old—for this moment.

Once, stopping to load again, he listened for the sound of Cobb's gun, but heard nothing.

As they kept coming he stood on the beach path firing toward the field, dropping birds for perhaps thirty minutes until his ammo started running out. The morning sun glared at him, but he glared back and, once, he made an impossible long shot on a bird so far away that he knew he'd never go look for it. It went down on the horizon like a stone.

He killed birds until he felt like a man who possessed the day, himself, and pure nature. A deep exhilaration boiled up inside him and he knew it was the greatest feat of shooting he had ever heard about, a hunter's dream, and a story he would later tell.

And still the birds came on, dark flights of them, coming in clusters and very fast. He kept firing until his ammo was gone, but with his last shot he got a double, feeling heroic and blessed.

When his shotgun was hot and empty he let out a yelp of raw pleasure.

descant

As he trudged into the field once again to pick them up, he heard for the first time the report of Cobb's gun somewhere to the east: a single, rather forlorn little bump of sound.

He picked up fifty-three birds.

On the long walk back toward the shack the pouch became a steaming burden, but his thoughts were pleasantly addled at what he had done. He didn't mind the weight. As his eyes drifted over the grey waters of Baffin Bay even that pitiful sight looked curiously beautiful in the September sun.

At the shack he cleaned the birds the way Cobb taught him: pushing out the breast of each bird with the pressure of his two thumbs, then tossing the bloody carcasses away. Jackdog remembered seeing old man Garza doing this with one hand: his thumb squeezing a dove's breast up and out. It was generally agreed that a dove's legs and thighs weren't worth anybody's trouble.

Jackdog tossed the remains of the dead birds down a dusty slope onto the beach: feathers, gore, all of it in a messy pile for scavengers to clean up. Afterward he washed at the tap beside the rickety porch of the shack, then started a camp fire with twigs and driftwood.

Cooking up the birds: the last of a tradition. In the old days the Garzas and other workers joined the Yoders in an evening picnic on the first day of dove season. The men cooked for the women. Today was a pale reminder of those times: a single skillet now, a midday lunch, no dogs, no older brothers, no women, no Garzas, just the old man and himself. Resenting it, Jackdog peeled two potatoes and opened a can of salsa, then went to the truck, removed the cooler, and opened a beer. Gliding over the waters of the bay two gulls called to each other.

He thought about his mother. She kept all of Cobb's books, doing all the complex accounting, and in recent years had even started making the deals with the cotton gin. A slender woman, shrewd and tender, she left Cobb to his nights at the Inn and to his days running around the countryside in his pickup. His sexual demands were long over, but his gruff complaints still bore down on her, so she earned what she had from the marriage. Jackdog remembered how she sat in the stands two years ago when he still played football: her hands over mouth, her eyes worried.

Cobb appeared, coming toward the beach through the furrows.

"Just got two damned birds," the old man announced, glancing at the sizzling skillet. "You get some?"

"A few," Jackdog admitted, and he nodded toward that steep pathway to the beach littered with feathers, blood, and scrawny necks and wings. Cobb shuffled over for an indifferent look.

"I betcha didn't put all the breasts in plastic sacks," he managed.

"They're in the cooler warmin' up your beer."

"And what're you cookin' for?"

"Lunch," Jackdog replied, biting off the word. In spite of himself, his anger flared up again.

"Well, it's too hot for a big meal," Cobb said, and he wiped down his shotgun and placed it in its leather case. "Hear what I'm sayin'? It's too hot to eat."

"Want me to clean your two birds?"

"Why, hell no," Cobb answered him, and he tossed both birds down the pathway toward the others. "I'm takin' the truck back to the house, so I reckon you can eat by yourself, if that's what you want, then walk back."

That did it for Jackdog. He rose from tending the fire, then kicked hard, sending the skillet flying. Hot grease and dove meat scattered around the yard.

"Now that is one asshole thing to do," Cobb told him, but before he could say anything else Jackdog pounced on him, turned him, lifted him by the scruff of his hair and the seat of his pants, and hurled him into that gory mess of dead birds. Cobb didn't stop rolling until he hit the beach, but he bounced up quickly, muddy, a smear of blood—not his own—on his reddening cheek.

"You ungrateful little bastard," Cobb spat out as he started back the same way, his boots sliding over the wet feathers of the dead birds.

"Come on up," Jackdog said evenly. "Raise a hand to me like you did to Mama and I'll break it off for you. Complain one more damn time and I'll close your mouth. You've had your run."

Cobb clawed his way back into the yard, but was short of breath. While he sputtered and gathered himself together, Jackdog had hold

descant

of him again. This time he sent the old man flying backward down the same slope.

"I ought to make you live out here in the same shack where you put grandfather," Jackdog told him. "But I don't want to see that much of you. You can move into one of them smelly rooms above the Inn. Better yet, move your ass into Kingsville. Into some damn condo. Come out for Sunday dinner if you want to, but tell me when you're comin' so I'll be gone."

He spoke smoothly, everything natural and impromptu, fluid, like the shooting of so many dove in the morning sunlight.

Cobb flailed around on his back down in the slime.

"And don't try to money whip us 'cause Mama knows what's in the books—all the shit you've tried over the years—and I'd just as soon send your sorry ass to jail. You don't know the IRS from a bottle of Shiner. You don't even know cotton fanning these days and that's why I'm takin' it over! Because I still know how to work and I'm sober enough to keep the damned farm in the black!"

Cobb made his way through all those little corpses again, wheezing, his face swollen with anger. He had a muddy stone in his fist and meant to use it.

"You've never had a friend or worker you've managed to keep," Jackdog went on. "If I can get Tony Garza out of the army and back we'll show you some goddamned cotton farming. Treat your workers right and they'll show you a profit, you dumb, sorry, tight-fisted old fart!"

Cobb cocked his arm with the muddy stone and stumbled forward, but Jackdog had him again. He used Cobb's weight against him, dodging his feeble swipe, then caught him in the crotch, lifted him fully off his feet, and hurled him over the side of the embankment for the third time. At the bottom, covered with sticky feathers, his white hair rumpled, Cobb lay back to rest for a spell.

"You can't even go up the right fence row," Jackdog said, standing at the edge of the yard and peering down at him. "You chased off two sons who worked themselves to death for you! One of 'em's ten times brighter than you are and what's he? A tractor salesman! And what're you? A big assed braggart who wore out the first Mrs. Yoder like you wore out the dogs! And my own mama, too, except she's too gentle to tell you so, but I will! Fuck your sorry ass! Get back up here so I can throw you back down where you belong!"

"I'm real partial to dove and you went and ruined a whole skillet of 'em," Cobb managed.

"Don't talk to me about dove! I shoot half the birds in Kleberg County and what do you do? Lay around on the beach!"

"I didn't elect to come down here," Cobb quickly added.

"If I ever let your miserable face back in the house, keep it locked away in your room!" Jackdog told him, and in spite of the tone the old man heard some small possibility.

"Well, sure, your mama don't want me sleepin' in her room. Where else do I stay put except my own damn room?"

"You should apologize to her every day for the rest of your sorry life! And get down on your knees and apologize to both my half brothers! And ask the Garzas to forgive you for all the shit you dumped on them! I'm deeding them land we've cleared and some we haven't because, by god, they've earned it. And before you die you can kiss my ass!"

Cobb sighed heavily and struggled to his feet once more. "Now here I come, so don't keep yourself so riled up. You could hurt a man carryin' on with such a terrible temper as I see you've got."

"Whenever you step outta line I intend to whip you like a dog," Jackdog informed him. "And you're outta line anytime I say."

Cobb clawed his way up the incline once again, then stood before Jackdog winded and flushed. In time he picked up the half cooked breast of a dove, brushed it off, and seemed content to keep it as a souvenir.

"How about a beer?" he asked, trying to concoct a grin.

"Why don't you walk down to the Inn and get your own," Jackdog told him "I worked all night icing down the cooler, packed gear, laid out food and ammo, then started lunch, but you didn't appreciate any of it. Take care of your own damned requirements. Later, if you're too drunk to walk home from the Inn, phone home. Mama might have mercy on your lazy ass, but not me."

"Now give a man one beer." Cobb argued, as if this much might be salvaged from the day.

descant

But Jackdog gathered up the camp items, even the hot skillet, and tossed them into the rear of the pickup with a loud clang. Cobb followed him around during all this, pleading his case for just one single bottle of beer, just one bottle to see him off on his trip down the beach to the Inn.

"Ask me one more time and I'm stuffin' you down the bird slot again," Jackdog finally snapped at him. With that he jumped into the truck, started the engine and drove away. When he glanced in the rearview mirror he saw Cobb—his mouth tight and sealed—as he turned his footsteps toward the Inn.

By the time he drove the mile back to the house Jackdog's thoughts had returned to shooting dove: a great day, a glorious series of wing shots, impossible shots, five birds with two barrels, a closing double, and he felt his jurisdiction over the fields, distant waters of the bay, and the creatures of the air.

John Byron Yarbrough

Boiled White
—from *descant* 40 (Spring–Fall 2001)

    Mama ties a rag around her head.
    Standing over the stove is hot work.
       A big black iron pot.
       A long wooden spoon.
      A caustic cake of lye soap.
        On Monday night
   Everything dirty gets boiled white.

descant

Charles Harper Webb

I Named My Cat "Keats"
—from *descant* 40 (2002)

Because he was pint-sized like the poet,
Illness-prone. The first time he went outside,
An orange Tom cuffed him, and his head abscessed
To twice its size. Cockney John may have
possessed him then, or while he lay unconscious
at the vet's. Or did the surgeon-poet enter
through the draining tube stuck in the poor cat's head?

It's certain that—stretched in my lap, my hands
conducting the concerto of his purr—he said,
No, no, go not to Lethe, neither twist
Wolf's bane, tight-rooted, for its poisonous wine.
Within a week, he'd rattled off "Endymion,"
"The Eve of Saint Agnes," "La Belle
Dame Sans Merci," plus all the odes.

He'd sit outside with Kate and me, watching
Clouds dirigible across the sky.
The sun's last rays ignited them, while a pair
Of mockingbirds extemporised. Kate
recognized them first: Felix and Fanny
Mendelssohn. Toadily, my Southwest
Toad, turned out to be Georgia O'Keefe;

Charles Harper Webb

Nigel the hedgehog was Shakespeare;
Boris and Natasha, the Russian tortoises:
Tolstoy and Akhmatova. The red
Squirrel that planted peanuts in the grass
Was Van Gogh, and the purple jay
Screeching like a rusty hinge was Klee.
Tchaikovsky, Yeats, Bach, and Vermeer flocked

To my back yard, chattering. Even snails
And spiders, black tree roaches, caravans
Of ants proved to be artists, though minor ones,
Like me. First among us all was Keats,
Making us laugh with his "Mra-raa!" and "Tee
Wang Dillo Dee," the "amen to nonsense"—
Used if I got pretentious, fought with Kate

Over trivialities, or didn't pay
Attention as he caught flies, chased pink
Ribbons, wrestled his jingling mouse.
It was Keats, I know, who called the others
To my house, and convinced Kate to marry me—
Kate, whose love offsets my lack of genius,
And makes me capable of anything.

descant

Bruce Machart

Where You Begin
—from *descant* 42 (2003)

Sad to say, but dogs get killed sometimes. Take a city like Houston, four million people and all those cars, sometimes it's bound to happen, but if you're like I used to be, it doesn't bother you so much. Anyway, before this is over there's one less dog in the world, so in case you're not like I was, fair warning.

But if you're like I used to be, when your fiancée of five months gets home from a day of slaving for that lawyer downtown, the guy who cuts her a check twice a month for the privilege of telling her what to do and watching her cleavage go red with splotches the way it does sometimes when she's flustered; when she makes it through the door and finds you scribbling your latest on a legal pad, still in your boxers with the newspaper untouched on the porch in its plastic wrap, the classifieds still tucked inside without a single job listing circled; and when a few minutes later she comes half naked and frowning into the hallway, as red-faced and eager for her evening shower as would be a farm wife after bleeding a hog, you know you're history.

Kaput. Finito. It's over and you don't even ask for that ring back. All you think is, Well, dip my dog, because that's a quarter carat solitaire with not too damn bad color and clarity. Even so, you just let it go, chalk it up to a learning experience, like the time you bought a quarter ounce of oregano outside the Texaco station from a pock-faced Mexican kid with jeans about half fallen off his illegal brown ass. You chalk it up. You say, "That there's a loss." All it can be. Next time—smell the weed before you finish the deed, that's all.

But *this* time—this time, when Gloria Jean Thibedeux tells your worthless, workless leeching ass to hit the road and never even mind all that stuff about getting married, that's exactly what you do. You hit the road. You hit it with all the plop and flourish of a horse turd dropped from a disgruntled gelding on the downtown leg of the rodeo trail ride.

Of course, Gloria ain't making this easy. No, she's got to strip right down to nothing but pink satin and the soft white skin that's been penned up all day behind her *lawyer-want-some-coffee?* business suit, and when she tells you where to get off, it's suddenly clear that this here's no warning. Nope. Turns out you're on the receiving end of a full-blown pink slip, pink as those panties she's reaching back to pull out of her rear. Yes, sir, there she stands in some of God's finest creations: satin bikini bottoms and one of those clasp-in-front bras that even you can get right in the dark. Your Gloria, nothing else on but that ring you maxed out the plastic for, and for once you don't even think about the bills rolling in.

"Baby," she says, her hands perched on those breeder's hips you've thought at times might make any stints in the delivery room as easy as laying back for a nap on Sunday, "if you ain't landed a job out at one of them refineries today—that or sold one of your precious 'Drama in Real Life' stories to *Reader's Digest*—then it don't matter how it breaks my heart clean in two, you gonna need another place to stay tonight."

Nothing altogether new, of course. This ain't the first time. You've been warned before, maybe a dozen times over the past four months, and sure, you've been writing, but you've got thirty-three stories and so far not a single cash cow. And now—now there's no sense in begging, so you sit there for a while in the kitchenette, biding time with your elbows propped on the yellow Formica table top. The new story you've written—a real ringer about a retarded kid trapped underwater in an upside-down school bus at the bottom of a ravine—is almost finished, and guaranteed, you think, to bring home the cash money *Reader's Digest* is doling out for this stuff on a monthly basis. You watch Gloria's pale little hands and those wide-slung hips and somehow none of this surprises you—not the way she's staring, lips in a tight puckered O like you've farted and accidentally drawn mud in your drawers, not the way the a/c snaps to life in the attic and spills its cool rush of air into the room, not even the way four months back you lost your job at Exxon where you'd spent three years loading fifty-five gallon drums of Varsall into tractor trailers. Hell, not even the guilt-like squeeze in your conscience you'd felt growing steadily tighter

descant

when, to pay your share of this month's rent, you sold the old El Camino you'd had since high school. Anymore, nothing's a surprise, but they say the expected ain't always easy, and now there's that slow grandfather clock of a feeling you get in your guts, like your heart's swinging way too low on a thin wet string in the wide-open empty insides of you.

"You best snap out of it," Gloria says, flipping that long black hair over her shoulder, and you can't help thinking it—*looks like a horse's tail swatting flies.* "I'm serious as murder one," she says. "Piddle-farting around in your underpants. Home all day writing your little stories. Out with Jimmy two nights already this week doing God knows what. Sweet Jesus, legal pads stacked up everywhere. You can't even clean up after yourself, let alone scrub a toilet or do a load of laundry. Let *alone* take care of a wife."

"You better *go*," she says, crossing her arms over the mess of red splotches on her chest. "For good. Right goddamn now."

Still you're waiting, leaning on the table like it needs holding down and waiting until it comes, the end-all to your be-all: "Toot-sweet," she says, the thoroughbred Cajun twang alive in her voice, and you reckon that's all she wrote, so there ain't nothing left but to call your pal Jimmy Love, tell him to come do his duty as your only real friend, former coworker, and owner of the '92 Chevy truck that's seen you riding shotgun while drinking off no less than three major league cases of what Jimmy always calls the post-poon blues.

What happens next, you might say, is about as predictable and necessary as a toothpick after corn on the cob. There's your father's old army duffel bag on the street beside you and you're kicking the curb, flipping pages of your legal pad when Jimmy Love comes rumbling up. Reaching over, he swings the passenger door open and pulls the hairs of his mustache down over his lips with a cupped hand.

"Well," Jimmy says, "don't know about you, but I'm picking me up a little hint of that déja vu," and when you toss the duffel into the back and climb in he pats the two six-packs beside him as if they were the fair-haired heads of sons who'd just caught a greased pig at the state fair. "This make four?" he says. "*Damn*. Four women? In two years? And your sorry ass actually wanted to *marry* this one? Level with me, man. You having problems getting it up?"

Jimmy can be like this, all that sprawl-on-the-couch-and-tell-me-all-about-it bullshit. "Just drive," you say, slamming the door, because you get it up just fine, and besides, the details ain't none of his business. "Do the loop."

It's not something that needs saying, of course. All the elements are in place. Jimmy's behind the wheel, steering that old truck out of Gloria's rent-house neighborhood and up onto Hwy. 225 where the stainless pipes of refineries and chemical plants wind and shine under the evening's last dose of sun. With the black spill of their smokestacks, you'd swear they were bent on hurrying the night along. As for Jimmy, he drives with the Southwestern Bell Yellow Pages balanced on his lap, and when he accelerates over the ship channel, there's Loop 610, thirty-eight miles of five-lane highway that never ends but just keeps circling the Houston skyline from six or so miles out.

"We're on," Jimmy says, merging into traffic behind a dump truck with them Haulin' Ass babes on the mudflaps, and when he gets the phone book balanced on the gas pedal and checks the speedometer, he goes, "The Ma Bell cruise control's a go, you homewrecker. Let's drink."

You crack the window and out come the beers. The whole town smells flammable. "Yeah, keep talking," you say. "But I don't exactly see you settling down."

"Nope," he says. "Don't see me buying diamonds every time some coon-ass gets my dick hard neither." He swigs his beer and hits the wiper/washer. "Me and this Chevy, we can flat squash some bugs, ain't it?"

When you don't answer he pulls on his mustache and makes a clicking sound with his tongue. "Come on, now," he says. "You know me, I didn't mean nothin' by it."

You know Jimmy, all right. Here's a guy with—as he'll tell you—*a truck and some luck and on good nights a fuck*. A guy just far enough out of his mind to own the Exxon shipping and receiving record for blindfolded forklift driving—all hundred and five feet of the loading dock and down the ramp without ever putting on the brakes. Yup, Jimmy's got more bowling shirts than sense, but you've been knowing him a long time and when tit turns to trouble he ain't ever late in that truck. He's good people, Jimmy, never mind all his ribbing.

"Don't go to fidgeting," he says. "Relax and drink your beer."

You do, and it's not as cold as it could be, but it slides down just fine so you take all twelve ounces in one pull and watch the Texas flag flapping on the can as you crumple it with one hand. Yup, still Lone Star, because it don't matter that some pantywaist snow bunnies from up north own the brewery now—it's still made in Texas and you'd just as soon raise your voice in the Alamo shrine as drink some mule piss from Milwaukee. Gloria, you know, is wrapped in a towel a few miles back, and the can in your hand can't help but remind you of the dark beer she buys by the case. "Blackened Voodoo," she'd said, "from N'Orleans," and when she poured some into your belly-button once, it set you to tingling from shin bones to shoulder blades. It was one of the first nights, when the sheets were all crumpled up on the floor and she sat upright atop you, your legs pinned beneath those hips. And before she slurped the beer from you, she reached down, easing you inside of her, and while she rose and fell, tightening those magic muscles around you, you'd caught yourself thinking some pretty silly goddamn things—something about love, *love* for chrissakes, and how you might could get used to this. About how, when she lowered herself down on you, she made a little piece of you disappear in such a slow and painless way you didn't care if she ever gave it back. About how, because of that pool of dark beer in your navel, you couldn't see down to where way back yonder something had stopped and you'd begun.

"Time for numero dos," Jimmy says now, crumpling his first can.

It's practically instinct. Loop 610, thirty-eight miles round trip, six beers apiece. With the evening traffic thinning out, get that phone book just right on the gas pedal and you can figure on a steady 70 mph. Do the math, you get five and a half minutes per beer and, by God, if all's in your favor you'll still be thirsty when you make it back round to the ship channel. Then there's no telling, maybe a night at Frogs, the bar where the Exxon boys go after the second shift, maybe nothing more than twelve more beers and another half hour driving the loop.

"You still ain't given me the skinny," Jimmy says, wincing back the first sip of his new beer. "Was it the work thing again? 'Cause you ain't found a job?" Checking the rearview, he steers past a rusted tanker truck and all eighteen wheels are screaming to beat all, so he takes a swig and waits, smiling at you like maybe you're a sweet young thing he's grown suddenly fond of. "Go on," he says. "Ain't nothin' to be ashamed of, got dumped is all. Happens."

You're thinking, *You bet. Real deep, Jimmy.* But you know there ain't nothing to say. Should have looked for work today instead of doing all that scribbling. But goddammit, you think, this is some kind of story and she was getting a little uppity anyhow and then, well—*then* you're off to the races.

"I'm-a tell you what, Jimmy, this one's for real. This story, the one I'm writing today? Got this bus driver in it, and he been known to tilt a few back, you know? Well, kids ain't stupid so they take to calling him Boozer, right? And Boozer's first and last stop—this is down in the Valley, you know, long-ass bus rides down there—and anyway Boozer's first and last stop is this retarded kid. Small town, they ain't got one of them short little buses, you know? Them tard buses?"

A little chuckle from Jimmy now, and you know you've got him.

"So, Boozer likes this kid, right? Feels sorry for him and all, but he's a stomp down, pure-D-fucking miserable drunk, and he's already been about waist deep in the bottle the day it happens. What happens is this—got this part from the news last night—Boozer's looking back at this retarded kid while he heads out toward the ravine, making sure the other kids ain't picking on him and the like. He's cruising this long stretch of highway out west of Harlingen, nothing but red caliche and sod farms, and he keeps checking the rearview, looking after the kid when Wham!, there's this horn and old Boozer's way over into the wrong lane with this gravel truck about to drive right down his throat. And then—"

"—Then he jerks the wheel," Jimmy says, swirling his beer, "and all them poor little bastards break through the guard rail." He takes a swig and smacks his lips. "And off they go into the ravine and end up breaking their necks or getting knocked silly and drowning themselves."

descant

Jimmy moves into the right-hand lane around, best I can tell, about twenty-five Mexican folk, so help me God, in one old beat-to-shit Ford Tempo. "Must be going to Wal-Mart," he says, pulling on his beer.

You go, "How'd you know?" and he looks at you like all of a sudden maybe you're not answering to your own name.

"Where else?" he says. "Been to Wal-Mart lately? It's all Mexicans. You'd think piñatas was on sale permanent."

"Jesus, Jimmy," you say. "About the bus, how'd you know about the bus?"

"Like you said, man. TV news."

It smarts a little, this guy busting into your story when he's supposed to be listening. "Yeah," you say, "but in my story the retarded kid lives. Sure, he's pinned underwater awhile and Boozer's about ten sheets to the wind, but that's why it's drama, man. 'Cause Boozer keeps diving after the kid, just keeps diving and diving, coming up for air, and he can see the kid down there, alive and wide-eyed and pinned beneath one of those bus seats that's come loose in the crash. Old Boozer's gasping for breath, spitting water, but he ain't giving up. He keeps going down, diving again and again as the bus fills up higher with brown water, and the whole time his head's just swimming with a three o'clock drunk. He's maybe fucked up royal, but you better believe he's gonna save his little friend."

Now Jimmy takes the phone book off the gas and puts his foot down hard. "But that ain't real life," he says. "No one lived, you saw the news. Facts is facts. That's what your folks at *Reader's Digest* is after. 'Drama in *Real* Life,' get it?"

That's when it happens. You see it coming out the corner of your eye. Just as Jimmy looks down to get another beer, something dark and fast flashes across the on-ramp ahead, then another something darts across, this one bigger, and by the time Jimmy pulls his head out of his ass you're bracing yourself—elbows locked—while the truck rears back and the tires smoke and Jimmy's standing on the brake. And then that sound comes. Not the squeal of the brakes, not the smack of that big black dog against the grill of the truck. Hell with that, you don't even hear that stuff. No, sir, if you're like I was, what you hear is the man screaming from the side of the highway, *No!* and *God No!* and *Oh no!* over and over while the dog slides away from you on its back, its thick black fur peeling on the concrete, rolling up like wet carpet under the poor damn thing while it slides and slides and keeps on sliding. And then Jimmy's got the truck over to the shoulder and he's throwing empties under the seat, saying, *Holy shit* and *Stupid dog* and *Great Goddamn* while you're zeroed in on the man who's walking toward you now with his face—no shit—actually buried in his hands, and you start to put the pieces together.

There's the guy's truck on the feeder, all jacked up with its hazards on and a tire leaning against the rear bumper, and then there's the dog, now still and limp and backing up traffic and not even alive enough to regret chasing whatever it was that must've caught its eye.

"*Yow,*" Jimmy says. "You all right?"

You and Jimmy been friends a long time, but still you tell him to *shut up,* just *shut the fuck up,* because there's this man coming up to the truck, and it don't matter at all what else is real or fake. Because it don't matter if he's got a wife or kids or a fiancée that's given him the boot or nothing. *Shut up,* you say, with a hand on Jimmy's chest, because outside that man is stopped now and kneeling on the asphalt shoulder and there's nothing else to say but that he's coming undone on the side of the road, crying for a dog he loved a whole damn lot, and well, when it comes right down to it, if you're like I was you've never felt like that, and all you know is that the whole thing makes it feel like that little heart has quit swinging inside you—only you don't know how, because you feel all tore open and exposed to the elements and there's traffic blowing by like mad and wind pushing in the windows thick and fast, the way that brown water must've poured in on Boozer, and the sound it makes is all muddled and crazy and broken to bits like the prayer you can't quite piece together inside you, the one that says, Please God, someday, let me have that much to lose.

descant

Dana Roeser

Land of the Lotus Eaters: Sea Island, Georgia
—from *descant* 42 (2003)

    Corpses I once
        dreamt about,
    at an amusement
        park, on a carousel,
    somnambulant
        in the gauzy
    September light, their
        skin weathered,
    their eyes tumbled like
        stones by
    the ocean air—imparadised
        on the seaside
    patio with baby greens,
        smoked oysters,
    stuffed crab. . . . I
        think of them
    as I drive inland
        through dry, red
    clay, the sad, deeply
        sad South,
    laden cotton
        fields, a kind of
    heavy snow resting
        in the furrows. Peach
    trees, pecans, turpentine and
        timber . . . overflowing
    logging trucks around us
        on the road, their
    load held on, it appears, by
        velocity, or

Dana Roeser

gravity, stripped trees
    that recently
were singing, that
    still chirp and
creak when
    the truck stops.

The lotus eaters don't
    travel this way
in a station
    wagon on
secondary roads
    with fighting kids
in the back. They
    spin between
continents, vacations,
    endless linen
and silk poised on
    hangers . . .

This grimy
    car, Georgia
and more
    Georgia, and finally
rural Georgia at
    the other end of
the state, our scrubby
    town, subdivision,
then the house
    reeking like
a kennel. My old life—
    that still chirps
and creaks when the
    car stops . . . a
breath, a flame,
    a shadow.

descant

Ronald E. Moore

The Real Funeral
—from *descant* 42 (2003)

When the suits and the dresses and the preachers went away,
we had the real funeral, my brother and I sitting in the gravel
of a town we'd shaken off long ago.

We got there just as Fatboy and his gravedigger friends were
finishing their job. They were sweeping around their
newest grave, the place that was our father's last one.

They didn't seem surprised that we came back.
One man drove by and said, "Your daddy was a good one,"
but soon had the respect to go away.

In the silence made heavy by our grief, my brother finally said,
"Dad, I'm gay." I said, "Mother, I didn't love you, but you
had my respect," two long-suppressed benedictions.

We wondered aloud how far apart they were, so Fatboy
measured, told us twenty-one inches. It seemed about right.
The gravel, the grave and Fatboy in a small Alabama town.

When they were ready to leave, Fatboy turned to tell us,
"Think of it like putting a coat in the closet."
It was the best thing anybody said that day.

We stayed until we both felt calm begin to spread,
then we walked back toward the useless, emptying house.
That was the way we closed the door.

Chris Ellery

Bimaristan Arghun
—from *descant* 44 (2005)

The Bimaristan Arghun, or "Arghun's Hospital," was established in 1354 by Arghun al Kamili, Mameluke governor of Aleppo (Syria), to house violently insane inmates. Situated in the heart of the old city, the asylum is designed around a central fountain, the sound of which was thought to be therapeutic to the prisoners, who were chained in complete darkness.

>The wealth and benevolence of Arghun al Kamili
>provided here for the dangerous insane
>an asylum of darkness, water, bread, and stone.
>The walls have absorbed their wails, their stench,
>their outrageous laughter in a honeycomb of cells
>like the chambered heart of Aleppo.
>
>This organ leaks into the lanes and suqs,
>arteries of color and life unchanged since Arghun.
>The devout still pour into mosques to pray,
>and merchants bargain over blood-dyed rugs
>and polished gold, brighter than the sunbeams carved
>in sandstone arches in the "house of patients."
>An old man reclines near the door of a shadowy khan,
>greets the stranger with an ancient peace. Children sew
>in the sweat shops, or quarrel over soccer in the alleys,
>munch white grapes and pears at the stalls
>near Bab Kinnesrin with its four doors,
>its four desperate defenses.
>Women kindle fires to cook the evening meal
>in the very barbicans from which
>defenders of the city once poured boiling oil
>and shot their arrows into the hearts
>of other women's men. The smells of food

descant

and human waste, all manner of rubbish, blown
against old stones scored by chisels
of Hittite or Mameluke. Under the full moon
the first rain of October has broken summer's drought,
refreshed the night air, and turned the streets to mud.
A boy carries a baby with a dirty face.
A vendor clangs the lid on his pot of boiled corn.
From balconies hang ivy and grape, the metal doors
of the houses, heavy and austere
as the great iron ball which defended Bab Antakya.

The tourists hail taxis outside the Great Mosque
A minaret of the Citadel ascends
preposterously in the distance above
the modern pandemonium of the oldest city on earth,
my Aleppo,
which gleams and gushes in its busy, vital procession.
As the shops close, the old town goes to its nightly rest
as frantic in its ease as the pulse
of a soldier resting after indecisive struggle,
savoring coffee and *arghieleh,* though uncertain if
tomorrow's assault will *in shaa' llah* bring victory
or death or more of the same.

That loving soul Arghun al Kamili was wise among men.
Where life is thickest and most sweet,
we cannot be far from madness.

Bonnie Hunter

In a Cabin on the Cossatot River
—from *descant* 2005 (Vol. 44)

Condensation slips from the bottom
of her tumbler splashing to cool her bare foot
steam rises from a pot of poke sallat
mixing with the smoke of her True Blue 100
she dances

As she chops green onions to the beat of a
forgotten tune that rolls out of a pink radio
she smiles in the kitchen in this cabin
on the bank of the Cossatot, because
she remembers

dusty roads, Coke in bottles, fishing, and
her mother's cornbread recipe
as she drizzles bacon grease in to a baking pan
she opens the oven door
she feels

the warmth flow over her face
like the thick humid mist that crawls up from the river
to calm hot days in canoes
into sultry nights on the screened in porch
she breathes

descant

Catherine McCraw

Instead of a Wedding Dress
—from *descant* 2005 (Vol. 44)

I knew I'd never marry.
So, when he asked me to the banquet,
I bought a designer dress, so I could shine
like a polished apple in a cut-glass bowl.

The girlfriend wore
a tea-length, tailored, linen,
apple-green gown
with silver buttons big as quarters
spilling down the front.

The silk lining kissed her satin slip,
which whispered sweet nothings
to her pantyhose.

Nothing was borrowed, nothing blue,
and for one night, this unwed woman
in the traffic light dress
signaled every passing male

bite me,
I'm tart.

Contributors

Lee Abbott is the author of seven collections of short stories. His latest book is *All Things, All at Once: New & Selected Stories*. Abbott is a Professor of English at The Ohio State University.

William D. Barney, who lived most of his life in Fort Worth, Texas, was Poet Laureate of Texas in 1962. "The Killdeer Crying," for which he won the Robert Frost Award, is his best known work and the title poem of his volume of collected poetry. Barney died in 2001.

Coleman Barks, Professor Emeritus at the University of Georgia, Athens, is the author of several collections of poetry including *The Juice, Gourd Seed,* and *Tentmaking*. He is well known for his translations of Rumi.

D.C. Berry, Professor of English at the University of Southern Mississippi, is the author of *Saigon Cemetery, Jawbone,* and *Divorce Boxing*. He is poetry editor of the *Mississippi Review*.

Doris Betts, Professor Emerita of English at the University of North Carolina at Chapel Hill, is the author of nine novels and collections of short stories, most recently *The Sharp Teeth of Love* and *Souls Raised from the Dead*.

David Bottoms is a Professor of English at Georgia State University. His first full-length book of poetry, *Shooting Rats at the Bibb County Dump*, brought him national attention in 1980. *Armored Hearts: New and Selected Poems,* appeared in 1995. In addition to poetry, Bottoms has written two novels.

Jerry Bradley, former editor of the *New Mexico Humanities Review*, is Vice President for Research and Dean of Graduate Studies at Lamar University in Beaumont, Texas. He is the author of a collection of poems, *Simple Versions of Disaster*.

Born in Germany in 1920, Charles Bukowski published forty-five books of poetry and prose before his death in 1994.

Bill Camfield graduated from TCU in 1957 with a degree in English and worked as a writer with the one of Fort Worth's early tel-

descant

evision stations, KFJZ—TV Chanel 11 (now KTVT). Camfield was a pioneer of children's television, writing "Slam-Bang Theatre" and performing as the show's host, Icky Twerp. Camfield died in 1991.

Albert Howard Carter served as head of the Department of English at the University of Arkansas after World War II. In addition to translations, Carter was the author of a collection of poems, *For Magi, Shepherds, and Us*. Carter died in 1970.

Kelly Cherry is a Professor Emerita of English at the University of Wisconsin-Madison. She is the author of eleven volumes of poetry, eight volumes of fiction, and five volumes of non-fiction.

Tony Clark graduated from TCU in 1965. In addition to teaching at Scottsdale College in Arizona, Clark was an accomplished poet, essayist, and playwright. Many of his poems, as well as his best-known play, *Bat Masterson's Creede*, explore and celebrate the Southwest. Clark died in 2005.

Robert Coles is Associate Professor of African-American literature at Hampshire College.

Betsy Colquitt, a native of Fort Worth, earned a Master's degree at Vanderbilt before returning to Fort Worth to teach at TCU. Founding editor of *descant*, Colquitt is the author of *Eve, From the Autobiography*.

Jim Corder was a Professor of English at TCU from 1958 until his death in 1996. In addition to making important contributions to the field of composition and rhetoric, he published four volumes of personal essays that reflect his interest in Texas history and culture.

Clyde Edgerton is the author of eight novels, including *Walking Across Egypt* and *Killer Diller*, as well as the non-fiction work, *Solo: My Adventures in the Air*. He is a Professor of English at the University of North Carolina, Wilmington.

Chris Ellery teaches American literature and film criticism at Angelo State University in San Angelo, Texas. His co-translation of Walid Ikhlassi's *Whatever Happened to Antara*, a collection of Syrian short stories, was published in 2004. He is the author of a collection of poetry, *All This Light We Live In*.

Contributors

J. M. Ferguson, Jr. lives in Portland, Oregon. He is the author of numerous critical essays and the collection of short fiction, *The Summerfield Stories*.

Robert L. Flynn is a Professor Emeritus at Trinity University in San Antonio, Texas. A native of Chillicothe, Texas, he is the author of *North Toward Yesterday* and six other novels as well as two collections of short fiction and the nonfiction narrative, *A Personal War in Vietnam*.

Edsel Ford earned a journalism degree from the University of Arkansas in 1952, and, after service in the army, returned to his family's farm and became a full-time writer, publishing poetry and articles in the *Saturday Review*, *The New York Times*, and *The Christian Science Monitor*. He is the author of *Looking for Shiloh*.

Daniel Garza studied with TCU English Professor Mabel Major, who taught at the university from 1919 until her retirement in 1963. Garza's "Everybody Knows Tobie" has been frequently anthologized in textbooks for young readers and is often cited as a pioneering work of Mexican-American fiction.

Taylor Graham is a volunteer search and rescue dog handler in the Sierra Nevada. Her most recent collection of poetry is *The Downstairs Dance Floor*, from Texas Review Press.

R.S. Gwynn is University Professor at Lamar University in Beaumont, Texas. In addition to writing textbooks and literary criticism, he is the author of several collections of poems, including *The Drive In* and *No Word of Farewell: Poems 1970–2000*.

William Harrison, a TCU graduate, founded the MFA program in creative writing at the University of Arkansas. He is the author of eight novels, three collections of short fiction, and three produced screenplays. His most recent collection of stories is *Texas Heat*.

Andrew Hudgins, a Professor of English at The Ohio State University, is the author of five volumes of poetry and three books of prose. His most recent collection of poems is *Ecstatic in the Poison*.

Bonnie Hunter studied at Louisiana State University and now lives in Georgia.

Colette Inez, author of nine volumes of poetry, teaches in the Columbia University Writing Program. She recently published her memoir: *The Secret of M. Dulong.*

Ulf Kirchdorfer is Professor of English at Darton College in Georgia. His poetry has appeared in numerous literary journals.

Ben Kimpel worked as Professor of English at the University of Arkansas for more than thirty years. In addition to translations and works on Shakespeare and Emily Dickinson, Kimpel authored, with his colleague Duncan Eaves, *Samuel Richardson: A Biography.* Kimpel died in 1983.

William A. Kittredge was Professor of English at the University of Montana for nearly thirty years. He is the author of several novels, collections of essays, and short stories, many of which deal with issues concerning the contemporary American West.

Greg Kuzma is a Professor of English at the University of Nebraska, Lincoln, and editor of Best Cellar Press. Kuzma is the author of many books of poetry; his *Selected Poems* appeared in 1996.

Anne Leaton is a native Texan who has worked and traveled on four continents and has published novels, short stories, essays, and poems. Her short fiction has twice won her the O. Henry Award.

Denise Levertov published twenty books of poetry, criticism, and translation before her death in 1997.

Bruce Machart earned his MFA at The Ohio State University. His novel, *The Wake of Forgiveness,* was published by Harcourt in 2008. His short fiction has been anthologized in *Best Stories of the American West.*

David Madden is a Professor of English at Louisiana State University. He has published eight novels, two of which were nominated for the Pulitzer Prize. He is also author of two collections of short fiction and several books of literary criticism.

Catherine McCraw is a speech-language pathologist in rural Oklahoma. Her poems have appeared in *Atlanta Review, California Quarterly,* and several other journals.

Walter McDonald, Professor Emeritus of English at Texas Tech University, served as Texas Poet Laureate for 2001. He is the author of twenty-two books of poetry and one book of fiction.

Contributors

Ronald E. Moore lives in Fort Worth, Texas. His first book of poems, *Alterity*, appeared in 2006.

Joyce Carol Oates is the author of fifty-three novels and novellas, thirty-one collections of short fiction, twelve books of essays, and eight collections of drama.

Robert Parham's work has been published by *Southern Review, Georgia Review, Shenanadoah*, and many other journals. Nine of his poems have been nominated for the Pushcart Prize. He is Dean of Arts and Sciences at Augusta State University.

Jill Patterson is an Associate Professor of English at Texas Tech University and editor of *Iron Horse Review*. Her stories and essays have appeared in numerous journals.

Carol Coffee Reposa teaches at San Antonio College. She is the author of three collections of poetry, and her work has twice been nominated for the Pushcart Prize.

Dana Roeser teaches creative writing at Butler University in Indianapolis. Her poems have appeared in *The Iowa Review, The Virginia Quarterly Review*, and several other magazines.

Pattiann Rogers is the author of numerous books of poetry, including *Song of the World Becoming: New and Selected Poems, 1981–2001*. Her work has earned her four Pushcart Prizes.

Paul Ruffin, Professor of English at Sam Houston State University, is the author of five books of poetry, two collections of short stories, two novels, and one book of non-fiction. He is the founder and director of *The Texas Review* and The Texas Review Press.

Annette Sanford is the author of two collections of short fiction and a novel, *Eleanor and Abel, A Romance*. Her short fiction has been anthologized in *Best American Short Stories*.

Karl Shapiro published eighteen books of poems, three volumes of fiction and autobiography, and eleven books of criticism before his death in 2000.

Richard Snyder, Professor of English at the Ashland University and cofounder of the Ashland Poetry Press, was the author of several volumes of poems including *Practicing Our Sighs: The Colleted Poetry of Richard Synder*. Snyder died in 1986.

descant

Larry D. Thomas is the 2008 Poet Laureate of Texas. He is the author of eight volumes of poetry. Thomas has won a Western Heritage Award and has twice been nominated for a Pushcart Prize.

Robert Penn Warren wrote nine novels, more than twenty volumes of poetry, and thirty books of criticism and prose before his death in 1989. He was the first poet laureate of the United States and received Pulitzer prizes for both fiction and poetry.

Charles Harper Webb, rock singer turned psychotherapist, is Professor of English at California State University, Long Beach. He is the author of five volumes of poetry, including *Amplified Dog*, which won the Benjamin Saltman Award.

Robert Wexelblatt is a Professor of Humanities and Rhetoric at Boston University. He has published three books of short fiction, a novel, and a collection of essays, *Professors at Play*.

John Byron Yarbrough was born in Fort Worth and earned a Master's degree in literature from the University of Houston, Clear Lake. He has published poetry in several anthologies dealing with criminal justice issues. "Boiled White" is the title poem of his first collection.

❧ Acknowledgments

The editors wish to thank the authors and their representatives who gave permission to reprint works in this anthology.

The editors thank the special collection librarians at Texas Christian University for their assistance.

descant Fifty Years
Edited by Dave Kuhne, Daniel E. Williams, Charlotte Hogg, and Charlotte Willis
ISBN 978-0-87565-348-8
Case. $22.50